Clara Thinks to Us

A Novel of hope through the memories of an old lady

By Veronica Solorzano Athanasiou

To my parents

Table of Contents

Introduction 1
Meet Clara Díaz Rouzoglou 3
My first understanding of the definition of LIFE 5
Growing in paradise 7
Today 11
The empowering wristband… and *cachapas* 13
Food Intolerances 15
Back to Sunday 17
I was a happy child 20
Memory genes in action 22
    At 17 22
    As a child 23
    As a young adult 23
My children 25
I left the nest 26
I found myself 27
Pros and Cons of being undefined 28
Motherhood 31
Information overload 33
Time will pass 34
Australia 36

Working from home 38
Reinventing myself 40
Our island, Europe's guinea pig 45
Two years to understand 48
Doubtful parents were proven wrong 51
The 20s revolution 54
The Universe 59
George 62
Clara's room 65
Emotional cleansing 68
'Celebrityhood' was confusing 70
The beginning of The Wave 72
From Academia to Home manager 76
Pre-menopause and Hot flushes 79
You're the youngest you'll ever be today 80
It's all relative 83
Grateful for science 85
Rose 86
Mistrust and acceptance 88
Mum, tell me more…... 92
Fear is harmful 95

Nicole	97
Music	100
The Moon in a tri-lingual home	102
Migration waves: from crisis to love	104
George in 2025	106
"Banksters"	108
The Zinopoulos effect	110
My Spartan	112
Bubbles burst	113
Sunday's back	115
The Rise of Rafael Ruiz	116
And our island was finally united	118
Back to Venezuela	121
Small talk at Rafael Jose's home	122
Eduardo Tentoza	122
Rafael Ruiz Gil	123
Sunday asks another question	124
Women coming together: From Caracas to Sydney	126
Ralph	129
Rose is back for more work	131
Lipras and the domino effect	132

The End of Populism 134
Decisive sum of small efforts 136
Sunday brings Patty 138
Cats and the common good... 139
Diego, finally! 140
Mars and Venus collide 142
Social recognition and social classes 144
Rose is engaged! 146
Clara Díaz, Clara Díaz…... 150
Sunday in the Caribbean 152
A refugee of old age.. 154
Exile turned blessing... 156
Explaining Venezuela 159
Awareness and Polarisation.. 161
A sad example of how it took to the Arts 163
Apathy became Passion 165
One continent, one history 169
Susie, Ralph and the twins 171
Happiness shows 173
Acceptance through love... 175
Diversity enriches 178

Bioresonance is everyone's friend 180
There's no magic pill to healing 183
From individual to collective 185
Sunday comes to visit 188
Professional beggars 189
Victim of the inequalities... 191
Hatred led to love... 193
Global or personal?.. 196
Remembering Alexis 199
Meeting the one.. 201
George is back from Amsterdam 204
It took time but it seems I'll see it in this lifetime 206
Rose is here again 208
60 years young 210
I was paid to talk!... 212
More about the Wave... 215
In comes Nicky 218
Déjà vus 220
Accountability.. 222
My good is your good 224
It started at the schools... 226

From and to the land 228
Splitting families 229
Bye Diego and Nicole 232
Cheers to YOU 235
Sunday asks how Clara was in her 20s 237
My energetic 20s 239
    To toot or not to toot 239
    Underestimating simple house chores 240
Neuroscience explains a lot 243
Lifting others up was the answer 245
Tolerance and forgiveness 247
What kind of mistakes? 249
Migrant crisis solved 250
Youngsters raise their voice for causes 252
Generational improvements in parenting 253
We pass on the good, the bad and the ugly 255
Sunday poses 2 new questions 256
Feel pride on any path you choose 259
Hurdles to happiness 263
Venezuelans in the Diaspora 264
A human phenomenon 266

The Bride is ready 267
Sunday is back from Venezuela 268
I am done here 270
A letter to Claire 271
Irina Divina 273
Last but not least of the girls 275
To the grandsons 277
Tribute from George 278
Tribute from Rose 279
Sunday speaks for the grandchildren 280
Bye mum. You will always live in our hearts 281
The end 282
About the author 285
To the people of Cyprus 286
Acknowledgements 287

Introduction

This book is based on the author's life experience. It was written, as a cathartic piece, after an introspection that was triggered by the way her teen children perceived her attempt at entrepreneurship.

The book deals with matters which affect life today. The topics that have to do with health and wellbeing are grouped in an imaginary movement called The Wave. Clara is neither a spiritual guide nor a nutritionist. She is just a woman, a mother, a daughter and a wife.

Clara Thinks to Us is a novel of hope, as all the worries the author had at the moment of writing, have a positive outcome in an imaginary future. The novel deals with personal and collective issues such as
- parenting
- happiness
- ageing
- alternative medicine
- spirituality

It also touches on other topics such as Latin America's social problems, countries divided by politics and wars, extremism and European migrant crisis.

Fiction and reality intertwine, as the story moves from the memories of the past, to Clara's present, set in 2055.

If you want to believe that our world can change for the better, let Clara show you how it can be done. See how your own happiness and fulfillment play a key role in conquering peace and justice for all.

Meet Clara Díaz Rouzoglou

It's 2055 and I'm 88 years old. I never thought I'd lived this long! In the circle of life, I'm dependent like a newborn child, so bear with me while the cycle is completed. At this point all I want is to let you know how much life is worth living, even if you don't feel it.

I cannot talk or move anymore, so I'm very grateful for this machine that types my thoughts. How many things is humankind capable of creating? And yet, how miserable can we sometimes feel in our undoubtedly fortunate lives?

After speaking for years about 'The Wave for Wellbeing', my children have asked me to think about my life so it can be shared in print. My daughter, Rose, will edit my thoughts and I hope they will, at least, entertain some of you during your compulsory screen-free time.

It's funny how print has become fashion again, just like cooking on wood fires or grinding your own flour. Convenience was killing us and it took accomplished and renowned scientists to stand up and speak the truth for the necessary legislations to be passed for the better.

I was unknowingly poisoned by the very water I was drinking and my speech and movement functions have been tampered. My brain still works in many other ways and I have a loving group of people to support me. If you're not acquainted with 'The Wave', or you're not convinced it's the right thing to do, I invite you to read my journey and how we had to take some tough decisions, for the sake of our own children, at the brink of disaster for humankind.

My first understanding of the definition of LIFE

When I was 11 years old, at school in my birth country Venezuela, we learned that a living organism is an entity that emerges, grows, reproduces and dies. That was it: 4 actions defined life.

As I developed from pupil to teacher, the definition had increased to 7 actions including movement, sensing, feeding, respiration and waste removal. The more scientific list now excluded birth and death. At least, this time, they stressed the importance of food consumption by including it as a life defining action. It was a step in the right direction.

My childhood lesson of death following reproduction prevailed in my unconscious, despite having taught a more precise definition for 10 years as an adult. When I had my youngest child, I became aware that the next step in my life was... to die!

I wasn't going to have 10 children just to extend my lifespan! I had spent my twenties in search of a suitable father for my children and I was blessed with a wonderful life partner. What about those who never found one? What about those who didn't want a partner or decided to remain childfree?

The simple definition I learned at the beginning of secondary school was certainly not inclusive enough to define LIFE, and yet, it haunted my inner self and quietly nourished my latent fear of dying too soon.

My main concern was 'Who will take care of my young children if anything happens to me?' These negative feelings eventually led to chronic conditions in my body that were healed once I became aware and dealt with them.

I shared my path on social media with the relevant tag #QuestToWellbeing. It was through socialising both on and off line that I eventually became a speaker: People wanted to learn more about my experiences and I needed to connect with like-minded people. This was the beginning of 'The Wave'.

Growing in paradise

As I was growing up, I was encouraged to explore and develop my potential to the fullest: My dad was the breadwinner and my mum took care of the home and us three children.

Both my parents were scientists and educators. They met while studying at University and lived during the post World War II era. It was a time of unprecedented growth and development in Venezuela.

Many European professionals had moved to the 'new land' in the hope of a better future. The arrival of qualified lecturers and teachers in all areas of education benefited our country. The migrants, who weren't gifted academically, worked hard on trade, tourism or entertainment.

Our bakeries were filled with French style baguettes and all sorts of pastries and cakes in the best Mediterranean, Central European and Middle Eastern styles. They were run by migrants from Portugal, Spain, Italy, Lebanon, Syria and Asia Minor.

Our lives were also enriched with some of the best music teachers and sport trainers from Rumania, Poland

and Hungary, to name a few. My birth country became a rich mixed culture of unequalled advantages for personal and social development.

The children of these post-war immigrants grew up with my parents, who were exposed to their languages, their cultures and different life styles. These children spoke perfect local Spanish at school and adapted well to this welcoming society.

Many new public, primary and secondary, schools were being built and staffed by knowledgeable teachers, who were mostly from Spain, but also from any other country as long as they could speak the language. Even at University, for example, my parents had an Ecology lecturer from Italy and a Biochemistry professor from Hungary. I grew up being able to distinguish between Yugoslavian and Polish names, by their particular endings or sounds.

My parents admired the dedication and sharpness of mind of their Chinese fellow students and embraced people from all nationalities and backgrounds. Our own country was made up of a mixture of three ethnic groups: Aborigines, Europeans and Africans. For the majority of us Venezuelans, our ancestors belonged in at least two of those groups. This was expressed in the extreme variation within families of even a few siblings: an olive skinned boy with honey coloured eyes could have a blonde sister with green eyes.

It was a time of opportunity for many, as revenue from the newly found oil fields started to bring huge wealth for the government. These gigantic reserves and the development of the oil industry were a blessing and, eventually, a curse. The sudden magnitude of this income, as opposed to the history of slow growth from farming of coffee and cattle that preceded it, led to many investments in infrastructure, starting from the main cities, where oil profits were being managed.

Land workers and farmers of many remote villages and towns automatically moved to these developing cities with their wealth of opportunities and amenities.

Children from the countryside met up with children from the European migrants in these growing cities. There they could finish school and go to higher levels of education that would equip them, with tools, for a life their parents didn't get a chance to have. Many were becoming teachers themselves to fill up the growing demands in the education sector.

It was also the time of one, of many, cruel Dictatorships in which people had to concentrate on their own instruction and stay 'out of trouble'. Freedom of speech did not exist. There were authoritarian regimes in some European countries at the time too. During my parents' lifetime, those who studied and complied with what was required from them, at work, would reach a state of security and stability for themselves and their young families.

By the time I was born, in the late 1960s, a young democracy was ruling our nation. Alternative elected governments from different parties managed to lead the republic for almost 40 years. It certainly felt like paradise to me, as I was one of the fortunate ones whose family lived the dream of comfort and even luxury. We were blessed with healthy parents who dedicated themselves to give us even more opportunities than the ones they had. It was a simple formula: study, follow the rules and succeed.

Today

My granddaughter, Sunday, just dropped in to see me. I love the way she talks to me…

"Hi *Yiaya*. How are you today? It's so hot out there! You're lucky there's temperature control in here."

Yiaya is the Greek word for Granny. Sunday turns towards the screen where she knows she can see what I'm thinking:

"Hello, darling. I'm better now that you came to see me. I can't feel the change in temperature outside but I am more comfortable when I am cool. You look gorgeous!"

"Thanks, *Yiaya*. We went to the beach today, on the East side of the island. No sticky sand there. Would you like a foot massage?"

"Yes, please! How's your new startup going? You're such a clever girl! And…what are those shoes?"

"Oh, you like them? They're the new anatomic trainers that you can wear all day. They're so light and they adapt to changes in the foot with information from the pendant."

"Love to be able to see all these innovations. It's amazing what I've seen over the years."

12

"You should see how popular the interactive wristband is, *Yiaya*. We're hitting record sales again this month. My startup is growing so fast. I'm so proud!"

"I am so proud of you too! I can't believe there are still humans who doubt themselves."

"We're going to empower them, *Yiaya*, don't worry."

The empowering wristband… and *cachapas*

Sunday and her friends have created a wristband that can read the waves emitted from any human's body. It detects when the person's energy level is low and communicates with them. The program sends messages like: "Something is draining your energy today and your physical activity has been nil."

Sometimes by making the person realise they've been immersed in draining thoughts, they come back to the here and now and start feeling better.

I can't feel Sunday's foot massage but it's good for what is left of my physical body. It will keep me breathing for longer so that I can continue thinking and communicating via the MRW machine (Mind Reader Writing machine).

"How's your mum, dear?"
"All good, *Yiaya*. She's busy writing her children's stories. By the way, did I tell you I'll go to Venezuela at the end of the year? I'll go to see Yuruani river and hike to Angel Falls."
"That's wonderful! I did that with your *Pappou* (Greek word for grandfather) on our honeymoon in 97. I'm so glad you'll visit that magical place! Eat lots of *cachapas* for me, please."

"What are *cachapas*?"

"They're like pancakes made with ground, tender corn kernels instead of wheat flour. You should try them with grated white cheese on top and lots of butter!!"

"Sounds lovely. Now I will add a little something to your MRW program. You'll see..."

Food Intolerances

In my late 40s I was diagnosed with many food intolerances. I had to omit a fair amount of foods from my diet and, when I was sticking to the 'safe' ones, sadly I was found to be intolerant to some of them too!

In my current condition, eating is not an issue anymore, since food shakes are added directly into my stomach, but I felt like my life was coming to an end with all my eating problems then. I used to think: How will I survive if I cannot eat a balanced diet? What's happening to my gut?

As with many other issues earlier in my life, I did my research and came across a few clues: Leaky gut.... there were different optimal diets to help with that.... Irritable bowel Syndrome was more severe and also triggered by foods. All the options I came across had a common denominator: autoimmune conditions. I wanted to know what I was going to tell the physician whom I'd consult.

I had blood tests and visited a couple of doctors when I was suffering the most with migraines, chronic fatigue, colon spasms and, in general, gut discomfort. The medics dismissed my symptoms and the test results, as being inconsistent. That led me to search answers in holistic medicine, an approach that was gaining momentum but was not the main way to treat diseases, like it is today.

I had known all along that my immune system was part of the problem but I never imagined it was running on overdrive. I discovered that when I understood how a parasite organism that had been living in me since my childhood had taken its toll on my gut. It had altered my own defence mechanisms and could, eventually, lead to a number of serious autoimmune conditions like lupus, arthritis and even cancer. So scary!

Back to Sunday

"*Yiaya*! You are not listening to me. Do you want to sleep?"

"Thinking of *cachapas* made me go back in time and I was remembering my problem with food intolerances. I'm so grateful there was a cure and I could enjoy *cachapas* with butter after that. What are you doing on the MRW's computer today?"

"I have changed the program so that when you think of the word 'emoji' the angle brackets will open for you to think of an emotion. I have used the classic emojis you're familiar with like smiley, wink, kiss and so on."

"That's great. Thank you darling. I'm sorry I drifted away. I'm listening now. <smiley>"

"Hey! It's working. You're good!... I'll have to bring you Patty, our new cat. She's lovely!"

"Looking forward to meeting her. <cat> How's your mum coping with her hot flushes?"

"Oh, it's been fantastic with the wristband for maturing women. She hasn't gone through mood swings in a while, she said, and the sweating is almost back to normal. The only thing is that she still gets headaches now and again."

"Sounds better than when I went through the menopause. At the end of the day, quantum knowledge has really improved people's quality of life. Those who still struggle with relaxation can let the wristband make the frequency adjustments for them to feel better. After all, we ARE beings of light as no one can deny the existence of photon particles in our cells. What physicists cannot agree is on the source of the force that keeps it all in harmony."

"There's no doubt in my heart that something, larger than we can imagine, sends love our way. I still like to call it God, *Yiaya*. I've always been fascinated by the story of our religion. I like a good story with a happy ending and, as we discover more and more in scientific terms, those who believe, can believe even more, and those who don't…. well, we'll have to ask them! Some are so adamant about their disbelief that once they declare themselves as agnostics, "they ain't coming back!!""

"It's always been like that, darling *mou* (my darling). There's a group of rebels like your uncle George who refuse to believe in the power of something we will never be able to comprehend."

"I know, *Yiaya*. It's so sad. They don't feel it either…"

"Don't say it like that. It's not sad for them as they decided on what works best for them. We cannot assume everyone will be spiritually fulfilled in the same way."

"True! All humans are on their own path towards spirituality even if they don't admit to it. Being agnostic is a way to define their path, isn't it?"

"Yep! I'm so happy you're open-minded about the others and you're fulfilled with what has been given to you. One of the great lessons we have all learned, through global connections, is that we can be different and respect each other's beliefs. They define where each person belongs, giving us that sense of immediate community which enhances our day to day development."

"Individual, community, world. Like our kindergarten song: 'you are the world, make it work, make it strong...' Right, *Yiaya*, I'm going to love you and leave you. Keep thinking and writing. I'm going to get a lot of income from your thoughts one day."

"I hope so! Bye Sunday dear. I love you too."

I was a happy child

I was an easy going child, compliant and adaptable. I was fortunate to inherit traits that allowed me to enjoy what I had. I know that my brothers' genes were different and they perceived their reality through different filters. Luis and Tomas are my younger brothers.

I was always jealous of Luis since my dad stopped playing ball with me, his first born, when the boy came along. Luis adored me and was always copying me in the best little brother fashion. I ended up apologising to him, in my thirties, for having been a mean big sister and he said he couldn't remember any of that. Phew!

Tomas was born 5 years after Luis, when I was eight, so he was more like a toy for me. I never felt threatened by him and always wanted to protect him. Somehow our characters were more aligned and we eventually became the Europeans of the family, while Luis remained over in the American continent.

As the daughter of 2 scientists, I was always a strong believer in Genetics. I was fascinated by how genes determine not only the colour of our eyes, hair, skin or the shape of our chin, but also our fears, hidden ancestral memories and our personality. All I ever wanted to study was that intriguing science, since the first time I came across it at school.

We now know that the ability to feel happiness, or sadness, is not only determined by our genes but also by how we've been trained to switch them on or off. Hormones, neurotransmitters, you name it, they all play a role in our emotions and perceptions of the world.

I also embraced epigenetics as soon as I heard about it. I understood that the visions, some called 'from past lives', are just vivid memories that our ancestors passed on to us. In a 2015 study, they found how fears and stress were more common in descendants of genocide survivors than in people, with similar background, whose ancestors were not persecuted. This means that we also inherit genes, already activated, from our ancestors.

Memory genes in action

At 17

At 17, I won a scholarship to attend a 5 week summer camp in Rehovot, Israel. I was the first non-Jewish Venezuelan recipient of such an award.

While there, we went to visit an ancient site with a few structures that resembled shallow and rather wide wells. The guide who was showing us around asked: "What do you think these were used for?" We had no clue! He insisted: "Look at them carefully and tell me what you think they were doing here."

Guess what? This girl from South America said: "To make wine". I had a flashing vision of people stepping on grapes, collected in these vessels, as part of wine-making. At the moment I spoke those words, I thought it was obvious because of the films that I had seen about the life of Jesus and ancient Rome. Now I know it was my '*Marrano*' genes speaking.

'*Marrano*' was the name given to the Jews, living in Spain in the 15th century, who were forced to convert to Catholicism. My father's family names were amongst those of '*Marranos*' once published by the Spanish embassies.

The guide was impressed by my answer. He asked me if I had been there before and I just said: "I've seen it in films." But later I understood it was a flashback in my unconscious memory from one of my ancestors.

As a child

I also remember as a child, less than 5 years old, how I absolutely loved an outfit that resembled that of a 16th century lady mounting a horse. It consisted of black leather boots, pantaloons under a slitted long skirt and a blouse with round lace collar and fitted sleeves. That must have been a memory from my French ancestors on my mother's side.

Word of mouth stated that my maternal great great grandfather came from France and entered our South American paradise via the Orinoco river, in Venezuela. They then translated their French surname to Spanish, to blend in with the other colonisers, in the late 18th century.

As a young adult

I always felt attracted to French things. In my mid 20s I eventually went to Paris to visit my brother Tomas. I felt like I belonged. The empathy with the people there may have been due to my inherited memories, from my French ancestry.

I could communicate in French after only a short course in my native Venezuela. Clara and France were a match made in heaven.

My children

I can see how genes are displayed in each of my 3 children: Diego, Rose and George.

Diego is the male version of myself. He reacts like me in so many ways!

Rose is a female version of her dad both physically and in the way she approaches life.

George, the youngest, is a similar version of my younger brother.

Their characters are spiced up with traits from grandparents and some aunts and uncles, but who they are, is ultimately a result of their personality and own life experiences.

I left the nest

25 long years had to pass for me to fly the nest. I didn't have the courage, earlier in life, to spread my wings and start my own adventure. I stayed with my parents longer than any of my siblings did. That's just the way it was and, at 88, I don't want to think about how different life would have been if the timing of my leaving had been different. I left the nest and went on my quest to happiness once I had conquered my freedom. Or so I thought.

I was only 16 when I finished secondary school and my parents didn't support the idea of sending me abroad to study for my first degree. It took 7 whole years to complete it, due to strikes at the University, in Venezuela. There, the standard of teaching was high but the management was poor. I then had to wait for my turn to apply to an educational loan, to pursue postgraduate studies abroad, and that took another 2 years.

In those 9 years I really grew up. I had worked as an assistant teacher and later as a lecturer on Statistics, a discipline I wanted to specialise in for a future career, possibly, in academics or research. I was accepted in a university, in the UK, and boarded that plane with my loan in hand and all my papers in order. I couldn't have been happier.

I found myself

Having an amenable personality held me back, many times, from experiencing what I desired. What it did ensure was that I was following the rules and, if something went wrong, it wouldn't be my fault.

I lived my first 25 years 'by the book'. The definition of 'book' changed through the stages of my life and, naturally, during my teens I searched for answers away from home. As a believer in knowledge, I bought books about everything, from sexuality and changes in the body, to achieving success and finding happiness. It took me 2 years, away from the nest, to find myself, and I finally did.

Pros and Cons of being undefined

I remember a statement I made at 17, when I was at the international Summer Camp, in Israel, with other high school graduates. On one of the evenings, we gathered around the campfire and we were asked who we wanted to marry in the future. I remember listening to the others' responses about their desired qualities: success, cleverness, handsomeness and the like.

I realised I didn't have a stereotype in my mind. When it was my turn, and I had to come up with an answer, the only thing I could say was "Someone who truly loves me". How undefined is that? I now realise, that I was fortunate to marry 'someone who truly loved me', and the details described by others were completely irrelevant. I couldn't have foreseen the specifics of my marriage, ever!

Not having a defined model for a life partner is good and bad, since you can't have it all. Because of where I was going to get married, my parents couldn't participate in the Wedding plans. My father never said he was looking forward to the day he'd walk me down the aisle - and in the end he didn't! He did walk me out of the car, together with my mum, each at one side, to the door of the Church. I walked down the aisle by the arm of my bridegroom. This is the way things are done here, in my adoptive Mediterranean island.

My mum never mentioned how she'd love to see me trying dresses for the occasion - and she didn't! My parents shared a vision, for me, of finding love in a person I admired and could respect, as the foundation for a good and strong marriage. The specifics were never discussed, which gave me the freedom of choice. Not having a commitment to marry in a particular geographical area, or under particular circumstances, allowed me to embrace other options that eventually led to the most fortunate decision.

I was living in Scotland at the time when he proposed to me. I went to Edinburgh to buy the Wedding dress I always dreamed of, wishing that my mother could have seen me trying it on, but knowing that she would like the one I chose.

I lived every moment to the fullest and with a sense of accomplishment. I had found Mr Right, decided to get married in his homeland, in his Church which I embraced as mine, and his traditions. I was living what I had wished for, 10 years earlier, around that campfire, in a nearby land. I had found the husband 'who truly loved me'.

My parents came to the Wedding and arrived after everything had been planned. They gracefully shared our joy and joined in the celebrations. I can only assume they trusted my choice, after all the guidance they had provided with their wisdom and, most importantly, their own example.

Motherhood

Not long after getting married, we were blessed with our first born, Diego. In my proper 'by the book' style, I read the latest books I found on pregnancy and childbirth.

How different reality turned out to be! I hated being awake during labour, as they performed an emergency Cesarean section, and I started choking due to what, I thought, were the effects of an epidural anaesthetics. It turned out to be intolerance to the iodine used to disinfect the wounds. It took many years of not being able to eat marine food, and a good bioresonance machine, to discover it.

I was so happy to see my baby emerge as I remained awake, but then, they didn't even let me hold him! Off he went to an incubator for 3 days until his bilirubin, and skin colour, went back to normal from jaundice. How far from what the books had described and from what I had expected!

In my 88 years I've told my son a few times: "The first time I held you in my arms and looked at you with all my tenderness you looked away!" We both laughed as he hugged me and said: "Ma!" We both know newborns can't even see properly. He was staring at the spotlights on the ceiling of the nursery. Nothing personal and another detail I hadn't read about in the books.

Information overload

One of the most enlightening moments of my life was when I read in an article, in the mid 2000s, that parents were under too much pressure, as they were expected to be informed about the latest trends to raise happy children. In the process, they would carry such a heavy burden that they wouldn't be able to enjoy parenting. Consequently, unhappy parents wouldn't be able to raise happy children.

It seemed like I was right where I never wanted to be as a parent. My goal had been to develop myself first, to be able to mother my kids without frustrations or resentments, and yet, I had fallen prey to the late 90s information overload. I was so relieved to know that it wasn't just me feeling the pressure!

Time will pass

I remember one day, while I was still the mother of two and trapped in my 'by the book' lifestyle, how frustrated I felt that the kids didn't seem to ever 'grow up'. My father called one day and I said: 'When do they grow up? I've been a mother for 6 years and they still need so much attention!'

My father replied calmly: 'Their dependency on you will lessen after a total of 10 years, more or less. You're almost there, be patient.'

I had misunderstood and thought I would have a break at some point. Ten years wasn't written in the books I read. None of the degrees I had obtained ever took that long to get. But parenthood doesn't have a graduation date. There's no degree to hang on the wall, no finishing line.

Good news is, my father was right about the children growing up. After the 10 years passed, they didn't need so much attention anymore. And we had the energy and the blessing to have a third child.

After my realisation that parenting was going to take 'forever', and that it is a full time job, with no weekends or holidays, I had the opportunity to take a break from being a full time Academic too, and I grabbed it.

Once I detached myself from my 10 year job, it took me 2 years to find myself again. Yes, I felt I had lost my identity with the preoccupation of my career and motherhood. I was doing so much, like many others were, but it seemed like the 'normal' thing to do.

I didn't realise how challenging my situation was until I moved to a far away land. It was a unique opportunity that life had presented to me once more.

Australia

In all the memories of my 88 years, this is the most important country. Australia taught me happiness is a choice, when the conditions are right. Australia is an isolated country, so far from both my homeland and my adoptive land. Moving there allowed us to see things from an outside perspective. And what an interesting exercise that turned out to be!

Australia showed us what was missing from our homeland: The sense of community. I can only say, as an analogy, that in Australia the tree is ours. In our homeland the tree is mine and in my birth country the tree is everyone's. This might seem simple but has a profound effect on the behaviour of the people and their perception of their surroundings.

Another thing I loved about Australia was its respect for multiculturalism. I was fortunate to live there when the Australian Prime Minister apologised to the original owners of the land, for all the abuses, from the past, by the Europeans who took over their land and lives.

In Australia, being someone's spouse was as good as any job title. I remember a fundraiser for breast cancer, in Sydney, where the speaker was the wife of the Prime Minister. They announced her on the screen with her full name followed by the words: 'Wife of our PM'. I had never before seen, that being someone's spouse, qualified as an occupation and was acknowledged as an equal.

I loved that no one ever questioned why I was a full-time stay-at-home mum, because many other spouses who had finished University, like me, had postponed or stopped their life in a formal job to take care of their children. Outsourcing childcare was rather unaffordable in Australia, and that often determined the career choices and status of many parents.

Working from home

After I left my job as a full time teacher, you could counsel, teach, train and participate in meetings, while being miles apart, thanks to social media and other online tools. In theory, you could make a living from clients you could find anywhere in the world.

Working from home was portrayed as the panacea for parents who wanted to spend more time with their children. There were special terms used to refer to people who were earning an income by multitasking on various devices, while being physically near their children.

I very much liked the idea of being able to use all my experience and knowledge while being a stay-at-home mum, after I returned to my adoptive island from Australia. I was enjoying simple nesting chores and I could feel the effect of the female hormone for pleasure, Oxytocin, released in most of us, while truly enjoying my home.

I started having free time, a year after I came back, and I had a huge desire to help others, in a true Australian way. I could use my knowledge of the local dialect to help members of the community with translation, to build a bridge between the locals and the expats. I hoped that, eventually, a source of income would appear. I just needed to gain experience. But this was not Australia!

Reinventing myself

Social Media channels were the perfect platforms to promote the beauty of this island. I wanted to help people highlight the local features that I had learned to appreciate, even more, while living far away. I needed to start somewhere, so I contacted the local English magazine and offered to do their Facebook marketing for free in exchange for exposure to the local businesses.

I remember one day a friend from my old job as a teacher came to visit and, when she saw my social profiles, she told me: "You are reinventing yourself." In a way, I was. Even though I had a clear feeling of what I wanted to do, I wasn't sure about the path I had to take. Nothing I had studied or experienced before could guide me on how I could succeed.

I learned about branding, elevator speeches, networking, the online world, leads, prospects and signing contracts. I tackled all these unknown issues as I used to do every time I faced a new challenge, one by one I researched and analysed them.

It was a time when having a vision and going for it was encouraged everywhere. I attended several offline network meetings on the principle that I had to 'keep moving' to attain my goal. I had never worked as a freelancer. I used to introduce myself as a person who wanted to help the community take advantage of the exposure social media channels would bring them. I was so used to writing résumés that my first elevator pitch was about 10 minutes long, instead of the one that was needed.

I slowly evolved into calling myself a Social Media manager and consultant. It wasn't until I attended many online seminars (webinars) on the subject that I felt worthy of such a title. After all, I didn't have a degree in Marketing. I just had the research discipline science entitles, and a very successful experience in public relations in Australia. It was a big stepping stone but I never really felt comfortable in the role. The '20 years of experience in marketing' bit was missing and this held me back until the end of this journey.

I never considered going back to University to get a degree in Marketing. I had waved goodbye to higher education when I left my PhD candidacy, in beautiful St Andrews, to marry Alexis. My number of years as a pupil and student totalled over 20! I didn't think I needed to enrol on any course to prove to the world what I could do. I couldn't even cope with the idea of an online long-term course. I had reached my capacity and I didn't want to waste time. I wanted to move on with real life experience.

After working as a volunteer, fundraising in Australia, I experienced a greater satisfaction of accomplishment than I had in my entire student and professional life. I wrongly assumed that, on the island, volunteering would be as respected as I felt it deserved to be. It seemed to put the islanders off. I don't blame them for not trusting such an offer. I never really worked out how the general thinking goes here, but I dare to speculate from this bed, that it's something like: "I wonder what she *really* wants." After so many foreign conquerors manipulated and imposed their culture on them, any degree of mistrust is understandable.

Once I gained confidence in what I could offer, I asked for a small payment from my first few clients. Charging too little made me feel undervalued given my qualifications but it gave me space to make mistakes as I was learning. I didn't realise then that Social Media Marketing was an emerging area and, even Marketers with a degree and years of experience, were testing the waters. I wonder whether, had I charged more, if things would have been different.

I learned another important lesson along the way: Offering unsolicited advice sounds pretentious to say the least. No one likes to feel patronised. Unfortunately, I was so focused on my final goal of helping local businesses take advantage of social media marketing, that I didn't realise I wasn't being asked for this advice until I had already said too much.

It became crystal clear that I had to stop and revise my work strategy. Initially, my garden kept me company, it helped me connect with mother Earth and it gave me the space and peace I needed.

One year passed, I improved by trial and error and a lot of research on the latest trends on social media marketing. I got better and made international connections in the early 2010s. I was having success, getting new clients and growing my online following. I couldn't have been happier. Vanity metrics (number of followers or subscribers, blog visitors, etc) can certainly boost our egos.

I had been praised as a teaching assistant at university, years earlier, for being honest and honourable. However, the real business world is very different from the academic world that I had experienced. Many times, perception is what counts in the business world, while in Academia you seek the truth and cannot pretend you've found it until you are able to prove it.

During 3 years I had made progress in finding myself and presenting this new Clara to the world. I still wrestled with the conflict between my academic background and the demands of the business world. And then, 2013 happened…

Our island, Europe's guinea pig

In early 2013 our island's banks were bailed IN by taking the depositors' savings in a most unprecedented manner. It was a bombshell to the banking industry that had been one of the strong players in the local economy. Needless to say, the lack of liquidity had enormous repercussions and my recent re-invention started to go downhill.

Some of the businesses I was working for closed down, others had to adjust their budgets and marketing expenses were minimised. I kept my prices low to help the locals, since their cash flow had been reduced. There were no more new clients coming on board as the consumers were in shock after what had happened.

The controls imposed on us meant that some people saw their savings shrink to the minimum, some credit cards were rejected because the issuing bank went bust and we didn't have the freedom to withdraw as much cash as we wanted. Even though these restrictions were lifted after days or weeks, the experience was traumatic enough to have an effect that lasted, at least, a couple of years.

In the months following the lift of the control measures, more businesses closed down, there was high unemployment, social benefits were reduced and the younger professionals on the island saw their job opportunities diminish.

Sadly, there were people working in the banks who were coerced into early retirement. I personally knew a man who had a heart attack from the pressure he had gone through, to make his final decision, to leave the job he had known for 30 years.

Architects, estate agents and building companies were other groups of professionals heavily affected by this turning point in the crisis. They had been affected since 2008 by the real estate bubble, so 5 years down the line, their hopes seemed to have vanished completely.

Macroeconomic indicators were just numbers until you put faces to them. Unemployment, inflation and a shrinking GDP, all had a direct impact on our lives. In our case, we knew people who had lost their lifetime savings. It was too painful to see, to hear and we couldn't do anything to help them individually.

The islanders reacted to the repercussions of the banking disaster in their own particular way. There weren't many demonstrations or strikes. People quickly put on their safety helmet and started picking up the rubble left by the financial grenade. They knew better than moaning. They had been through a military invasion of their Northern territory less than 40 years earlier in which they lost lives, homes, dreams and lands. This new challenge they were facing was unfair but not life threatening.

Two years after what was known as the 'haircut' of deposits, in 2015, people started to accept what had happened. They carried on with their lives, with whatever scars had remained from the experience, both in their souls and in their finances.

Two years to understand

Psychologists say you need two years to learn to live with a loss or any new circumstance in your life. It's how long it took me to understand and accept what seemed to make no sense, with regard to where we were living on the island.

When I came to live here, my husband, Alexis, welcomed me in the village where he grew up. I remember him saying, years later, with a big smile on his face: 'In my village, I am king.' I always wished I could feel that proud about my native city but I didn't live there long enough to feel like its 'queen'.

Alexis' village is beautiful. It spans from the Mediterranean Sea towards a dry hill, typical of the Middle East. There even is a lake that is a natural reserve for migrating birds. My perception of it now is very different from what it was back in 1996. It was not green enough, too dusty and the lake was way too dry, for too long, for what I would have considered paradise in my late 20s.

I started looking for a job upon my arrival. I found a teaching position in an English speaking school in the capital. The school was lovely but it was 47 km away from my adoptive village. I didn't mind the drive at the beginning, since Alexis and I used to commute together.

At some point, reality hit and I started questioning the daily 100 km round trip. For me, the logical thing to do was to move to an apartment in the capital where we were both working. We didn't have any social life in the village, as Alexis friends were scattered all over the island. Neither did we meet on regular basis with his family members. Everyone seemed to be doing their own thing.

Alexis would always get upset when I suggested we should move to the capital. He couldn't explain to me why he wanted to live in the village and nowhere else. I hadn't heard him say he was 'king' of his village yet, so that made it even more difficult for me to understand. Having experienced so many moves with my parents as a child, I was conditioned to live in the town where the job was.

It took time for me to learn the language and notice the use of the word 'foreigner' on people, I thought, were locals. Anyone whose parents had refugee status was referred to as 'ξένος' (foreigner). And it wasn't in a xenophobic or exclusive way. It was like a tribute to all the suffering they had gone through during the occupation war in 1974. It was a thread of hope to recovering their long lost homes and fields. Hundreds of thousands had been displaced from villages in the, then occupied, territory of the island and came to live in 'free' villages like ours.

The refusal of my husband to move to the capital was a simple defence mechanism not to be a 'foreigner' in his own country. This was a logic that I couldn't comprehend until I learned about the history of the island, especially from the refugees' point of view.

It took me 2 years to understand this new concept of being a 'foreigner' in your own country. Two years of observation and analysis helped us overcome this small hurdle to a more loving and understanding relationship. Two years were needed to sort out a disagreement between two people. No wonder it took so much longer for us, as parents, to believe that our children would take good care of themselves, the planet and us when their time came.

Doubtful parents were proven wrong

In the mid 2010s many parents doubted the world's future, as their children seemed forever dependent on the digital world.

I remember my children would spend most of their time at home in the good company of some display device. It was the time of entrepreneurship and startups, a great shift from the way we grew up and prepared for a 'better future'. But we all seemed to be chained to some sort of screen that would limit face to face communication.

Schools started to use these devices as teaching aids in an attempt to mimic the children's preferred way of soaking information. Many parents communicated with their children via social media messaging, even when together in the same house, to avoid waiting for the headphone removal in order to get their attention.

We didn't know whether we were doing what was best for our children. Was it really necessary to remain connected to the internet the whole time or would it be better to time-out from these devices?

Perhaps it was the gloom of the economic situation we were immersed in, because, contrary to our pessimistic expectations, our children grew up to prove that our fears were unfounded. They could improvise and care more than we ever did in our lifetime.

My generation, sometimes called generation X, seemed to talk about how to live a happier life and make the world a better place, but our children actually 'walked the talk'. I'm so proud of what my children and grandchildren have accomplished!

They managed to break that addiction to screens we so obsessed about. They used the screens instead of being used by them. I remember when the all-in-one pendant was invented: You could talk, watch, listen and remotely work your appliances from this magical device. It was OUR children who invented it in the 2030s. They made sure to cover it with a protective layer that guarded our bodies from the dangerous radiation involved in wireless communications.

They couldn't have done it completely on their own. Parents became more aware of the dangers of too much screen time and, as legislators were also parents, they declared compulsory internet-free periods of time.

All communication companies had to comply and they eventually designed a system in which each user had to spend 8 consecutive hours disconnected plus 2 hours in intervals at their own convenience. This was the parents' ally in controlling when children should sleep and in forcing them to spend time off the screens after school. The schools that had wireless internet connection were also regulated under subsequent legislations.

The attempt to replace books with tablets failed. Schools ended up having only one classroom with interactive tablets that were not to be taken out to other school premises. It turned out that giving unlimited access to the internet was too much of a distraction and the children learned better from old fashioned books, since they were the exception rather than the rule, for them.

Aside from the laws limiting screen time, free play time increased, allowing children to develop their creativity.

The 20s revolution

There was a game changer in the 2020s: Fear was conquered and the common good prevailed. The children of generation Z had grown up immersed in an ocean of information and knowledge. They didn't have to memorise anything, so once they had satiated their hunger for entertainment and dumb electronic games, they started to move and get fit physically, mentally and spiritually.

That was more than any generation X-er ever achieved. The children born after 1995 were leading the way: They didn't want riches or fame, instead they wanted a reason to fulfill their existence. They felt fortunate to live in a world that allowed more liberties than those in some countries of the Middle East and Africa. There were so many conflicts in those areas, that children were growing up there with too many limitations.

Our children grew up in a time of opportunities, with family trips abroad during school holidays. As adults, they already had a wealth of experience in travel, culture and living. For this reason, there was still room for them to move on to the next level of expectations.

There were countries where people felt they were lagging behind and they wanted a taste of what wealthier neighbours had been enjoying for longer than them. They immersed themselves into consuming when they got the chance and quickly got a feeling of what it meant to be enslaved by the insatiable need to buy. They could see themselves reflected in other people's lives, since social media provided 'Celebrityhood' for all.

Anyone with time, resources and a bit of talent could become an online celebrity and make money out of it. It wasn't a big deal anymore, it wasn't unreachable thus it became less attractive. There were YouTubers, Instagrammers, Snapchatters and new celebrities emerged on the 'coolest' social platform of the moment.

I reached capacity after a while and stopped trying to keep up. I was from the Facebook generation and that's it. It's like with everything in life. There comes a point where you don't want to make new friends nor to see new places or open a new social profile.

After abandoning entrepreneurship, I philosophised about the meaning of success. Then I went on to study history, politics, psychology and spirituality to fulfill my needs at that stage in my life. I didn't do it formally but rather using the resources that I had at hand: books, talks and the internet. Many people in my generation just remained receptors of information rather than seekers of the truth. The majority repeated like parrots what resonated with them.

The younger peeps were wired differently. They could face their fears, distinguish what was a real threat from fabricated propaganda and make informed decisions. A very important position they assumed was to bid on understanding between members of opposing causes rather than giving in to fear.

There had been many ambassadors for peace and education like Malala Yousafzai from Pakistan and others who dreamed of justice even from behind bars like Leopoldo López in Venezuela. Their voices rose above the noisy online world and they spread their messages all over the planet.

It was difficult for dictators to silence dissident voices and it was impossible for governments to hide how little they were doing for their countries. Malala and Lopez are just 2 examples of the first modern fighters for justice, like Ghandi and Mandela had been in their own time. Many more followed in their footsteps in other countries.

Conquering our fears on a global scale was not something that happened overnight, neither was putting the common good first. People had to develop, not only spiritually, but also physically and, even though this happened at a pace never seen before, it still took time to spread.

As the less fortunate searched for a better life, migrants arrived in places where they could find opportunities. The residents would either feel threatened or accepting. The way the facts were presented to them was paramount in what feelings would prevail.

We saw some free thinkers go out of the comfort of their homes and routines to show support and love to arriving migrants. It was the effect of seeing facts and listening to opinions, on social media, that might have never been portrayed on mainstream media.

Whoever paid attention to traditional broadcasting based on ratings, could see how bad news was always placed at the top of the headlines. It created fatigue on the audience and, eventually, sensationalism declined and gave way to a more balanced and objective way of reporting.

Individual choices had an 'en masse' impact on production of new programs. After all, media without an audience is worthless.

It was the same with the inclusion of the concept of spirituality in our lives. People's views of religion became less focused on radicalism and moved to a more open state. As a result, an understanding was reached that perception is formulated by people's unique character and this resided in each human obtaining a position regarding their own spiritual path.

The Universe

Some people acknowledge we are not self sufficient but rather that we need a force or energy to fulfill our human existence. They call it 'The Universe', 'Potentiality', 'Consciousness', 'Divinity', 'The Source', 'Master', 'Lord'.... There are also those who, at least, have a stand on the issue of spirituality by declaring they are agnostics. Either position is accepting of a concept that has been intertwined with humanity itself since its beginnings.

The last 50 years have seen a boom both in people looking inwards and also in caring for our planet. I remember in 2015, when I started my own journey inwards, as I fought my food intolerances, how the quality of the knowledge that we had access to via the internet was incredible compared to how things worked in the early 1990s. There was no need for trips to the library, or to a yoga centre or to a spiritual guide. All you had to do was to search online and there it was: asanas for beginners, meditations or prayers from different religious or non-religious views and all the scientific summaries to back up their benefits.

We all believe what we choose to. Sometimes we feel most comfortable ignoring our spirituality for a long time until, one day, we are ready to seek answers and look inwards. This might change from what our parents made us do as children to what we feel more comfortable with at different stages of our lives.

I personally found it fascinating how there were scientists from prestigious research centres who correlated their findings on quantum physics with a 'superior' or external force, or 'source'. Some even went to the length of finding biblical passages that would correlate with proven facts in this field of physics. The interpretations were many. What all did agree on is that they couldn't explain how these proven 'kind of magical' facts were happening. The Socratic paradox seemed to be as current then and even today, as it was when he stated 'I only know that I know nothing'.

Another fascinating discovery for me was that our cells communicate with each other and that there is measurable energy that emanates from the organs of our body. I found bioresonance to be a very useful application of this fact. It was my best friend in diagnosing my food intolerances and it cleared my body from the pathological vibrations those foods produced in my cells.

Understanding that the food we consume can fill our body with harmful energy was another very important breakthrough for me. Today people truly appreciate the value of those who grow the food that will nourish their bodies. Our individual choices had a direct effect on how agriculture and livestock production went back to more natural ways.

I remember the example of goats and sheep on the island. They grazed in the open fields as opposed to cattle that were kept in confined spaces and were being fed hay and seeds. Milk from the 'happier' sheep was less toxic because natural grazing meant fewer chemicals needed to treat infections and other complications from an intensive production system. Besides, good old chemistry shows that the human milk molecule resembles more that of goat milk than that of cow milk.

George

"Good morning, mum!"

"Mmmmm…"

"Come on Clarita, think to me!! You know I have a busy day, don't ignore me. I gave you a kiss and I've been here watching you sleep for a while but I have to make a move and didn't want to leave without reading your thoughts for me today."

"Hi baby *mou*…. give me a sec… how are you?"

"I'm good, mum. I'll be leaving to Amsterdam tomorrow to the annual flower and fruit show to see what's new."

"Oh, I wish the machine could send me images the same way it can type my thoughts, but we're not there yet…. You can describe them to me when you're back and show me photos. I'll give me my full attention, I promise! After the original forms of oats you found last year, I wonder what's next."

"I'll bring you something we can incorporate in your food shake. At least some cells will have a feast."

"I love you, my baby. Give my love to Susie and the kids."

"Love you too mum. Fingers crossed, I'll make some good connections like I usually do."

"I'll be praying for you then, as I usually do."

"Bye mum."

I'm so glad my George is a successful entrepreneur. He got that trait, lacking in me, from his father. I like telling him that I pray for him even if he doesn't acknowledge it. At least he doesn't get offended. In my heart I know he gets the love energy I send him through prayers.

George was born 10 years after our Diego and, that age difference, allowed us to experience the youngest possible generation as parents. He grew up with us, mums, glued to our phones, just like our teenage children. I remember he used to tell me off, just like I'd make his older siblings put down their own phones.

"Mum, please put the phone down. I'm hungry!"

And I'd listen. <smiley>

The resilience of the third child comes from the fact that, the parents, know they can survive certain hurdles and are, also, a lot more tired than they were when the older children were young. In our case, George enjoyed a more relaxed upbringing, as I had decided to slow down my pace in life by the time he was born. From my 3 children, he was the one who had more free-play time during his preschool years. He was a generation Z baby with a generation X mum.

All the kids of generation Z were never glued to their phones in the same way we were. For us, the X-ers and for the Y-ers, phones had evolved during adulthood or late childhood. For the Z-ers, they were just another gadget, like a fork had been to us. They were born with access to tap interactive icons, before they even knew how to read.

George talked to me unlike any of my older children and he demanded so much more from us as parents. It's like he felt he had missed out during those 10 years we were a family without him. We felt, as parents, that he was going to have 10 years less of our affection than his older brother Diego, so we conspired with him and gave in to most of his requests.

Today, George brings me 'superfoods' from his research for his healthy food delivery business. I cannot chew them, but they come with an extract he can spray on my palate, for me to get a taste. Sometimes they're not as good as the unhealthy flavours of my childhood, but it's interesting to explore new food territories.

Clara's room

This room has all the equipment it needs to screen my food intake. It hardly resembles what it used to be. At least these walls and ceiling witnessed better times during my life with Alexis. We used to look at the modern ceiling lamp and remember the roof window in room C26 back at the Hall of the University where we met.

The ceiling lamp is the only modern item in the bedroom. We built our house when I was pregnant with Diego and we made sure it resembled the kind of house I remembered from my tropical birth country. We fitted wooden cupboards and bought wooden furniture. It had a feeling from both our parents' homes.

Venezuelan houses had a lot of influence from Mediterranean architecture, so there were no disagreements regarding the style and the plan of the house. I did get a chance to see my in-laws' house before they tore it down. Unfortunately my mother-in-law left this world way too early and she wasn't around to keep the extended family together. Their house was dismantled and the space gave way to a new building in tune with the booming times that lay ahead.

Our bedroom is so spacious it can fit an extra single bed on one side, so there is plenty of room to place all the machines that monitor my vital signs while I am bed bound. It's sad that I cannot go out on the wheelchair anymore, but it would be too dangerous. I can still enjoy nice smells, and listen to music and to birds chirping outside when the weather is nice.

I enjoyed the days I could go out on my wheel chair. Somehow I always knew I'd end up using one during my late life stages. I always wanted a one storey house. Having grown up in a 2 storey home, I knew it could be a problem for a wheelchair bound person. We had enough space to build a comfortable home on a flat plan and the plot allowed for a basement to place the service area.

Now that Alexis is gone, my children make our bedroom as pleasant as possible. Rose is in charge of the music, Diego is researching with a new ceiling colour device and George tests the 'superfoods' to add to my feed. Sunday tweaks the MRW machine and I have Nicky to bring audios for me from the books I love.

I do miss touching the pine trees. They surround our basement and have grown as tall as the rest of the house. I can still get a glimpse of them by looking out of my window and smell their oil extract that George prepares for me. My eyes still allow me to see, my good old myopic, laser corrected brown eyes. I can see myself in the mirror and I am aware of my breath and my wrinkles. It is a blessing to breathe and to have so many wrinkles too!

I don't keep my social profiles updated anymore. There is a photo over 10 years old, from the time I was 75 when I stopped public speaking. There is a time to retire from mass 'celebrityhood' too. Those were the years I decided to become a full time *Yiaya* and to be available to my ailing husband and friends. I knew a few dark secrets from dear relatives and friends, and I knew my presence would comfort them in their older age, so I planned a few trips and went to help them take that heavy burden off their shoulders.

Emotional cleansing

Bad memories and feelings can very much disturb our health and our peaceful path through life. I knew a dark secret from a dear childhood friend who decided to interrupt a pregnancy in her early twenties. Years later, I thought of the burden she must have been carrying when I watched an episode of the series Sex and The City.

In that episode, Carrie described her feelings about interrupting an unwanted pregnancy in her early 20s, as she was in the waiting room with her friend Miranda, who would have an abortion. Miranda, thoughtfully and doubtfully, asked Carrie when the grief had passed. Carrie replied: "Any minute now." Such a powerful statement of how the grief never ends. My dear friend came immediately into my mind.

In a TV series or in a book, it is possible to change the ending before publishing. In real life, there is only one outcome that results from the choices you make. When I went to see my friend, whose secret I shared, we didn't have to talk about it. We both knew. She was 74 and already a grandmother to 4 gorgeous children, but she was still waiting for the grief to pass. Somehow, my presence made her grief a shared one.

We went for a walk by the beach one day and she opened up to me and said: "I've never forgotten my lost twins." And I said: "I'm sure they have forgiven you. You've mothered them through your other children and your grandchildren. Now you have to forgive yourself." We both cried and hugged, and she said "Thank you for being here to let me take this off my chest. I don't know how much more time I have but I will work to resolve this issue. I'm visiting my spiritual guide tomorrow."

After that conversation, my friend lived another 10 years. She wrote a letter to me 2 years after my last visit. Seeking forgiveness from our God had helped her forgive herself and become a better mother and grandmother for the time that remained of her in this life.

We have to love and forgive ourselves and seek help from our spiritual guides when the issue is as serious as this.

'Celebrityhood' was confusing

During my first attempt at entrepreneurship, the fact that you could create a virtual profile, that would attract followers from all over the world, was a novelty that confused many of us. I got trapped into thinking that because I was making new online connections, a prosperous business would follow. Nothing was further from the truth.

As time passed, there was more information regarding how to grow your business, how you should never, ever, give up on your dream, and how people had earned millions from a good idea and some hard work. Many of my acquaintances wanted to follow entrepreneurship. They were investing time and money in mentorship programs to find inspiration and guidance.

I followed those messages, I committed to succeed as a blogger and consultant, and, after 3 years, I was nowhere near my goal. I realized, after some analysis, that the missing bit of information was, that for every success, there were thousands of failures no one was talking about. We used to repeat Thomas Edison's principle, of never giving up because we could be so close to success, but this can also be seen as commitment bias. The key is to find the balance that makes us happy.

While I was still immersed in the attitude of never giving up as an online marketing consultant, my children Diego and Rose, who were 15 and 12, put a mirror in front of me with their poignant comments. I saw things for what they really were and decided to call it a day. Entrepreneurship wasn't for me and it is not for everyone, as it is widely acknowledged today. I just needed that little push to be honest with myself and admit I wasn't comfortable doing what I was doing.

I was hurt and I reacted swiftly by organising my ideas. I had to revise my goals. I came to the conclusion that there are no magical formulas to success. Sometimes you have to give up on a dream that is not feasible, and it is very important to listen to your gut feeling.

The change of direction eventually led to what I later succeeded at: The Wave, a feasible approach to health, success and happiness.

The beginning of The Wave

The Wave is about being honest. It is no cult or lifestyle manual to happiness. It is based on my life experience, a personal journey that resonated with many others but is in no way universal. The Wave encompasses what I learned about health, happiness, success, motherhood, living in an adoptive land and my attempt at entrepreneurship.

I started sharing my personal journey online and it seemed like many others were going through similar experiences. We simply shared our fears, findings, doubts, successes and failures, and the tools to overcome the challenges that we were faced with in life. My 'Wave' was just one of many in the whole world.

I had already tried Academia and left from exhaustion. I then attempted what many called 'mumpreneurship' or 'solopreneurship'. I left, even more tired, after realising that those are not terms you give to a person who is managing a home and a family. Just because we need validation from Society we must not force ourselves into another more 'productive' role, in the sense of some macroeconomic indicator.

One thing was clear to me: The roles of the 'homemaker' and 'being available' were underrated.

They had to be included as valid options for people who decided, or were forced by the circumstances, to pursue them as an occupation. It was not enough to have empathy amongst women. What about men who were playing these roles? I wasn't happy until I started defending my position as a full time mother, wife and home manager. The first person I had to defend myself from was me.

I had felt aligned with my role at home when we returned to the island, after having lived in Australia for some years. I was in charge of renovating the garden. I wanted to carry on with our social life the same way as in beautiful Sydney. I wanted to feel as fulfilled here as I had felt there. I was looking forward to using all the newly built facilities and taking advantage of the weather that allows for planning outdoor activities during many months.

There was only one problem: It wasn't as easy to get together with friends here. I had thought that because life is simpler on the island, all would work out the way I had imagined. But ladies reacted differently to champagne in the morning. There was no chance to enjoy lunch together because school finished a lot earlier here. It seemed like we were forced to spend countless hours in the kitchen, serving our picky eaters. They had to be collected from school at lunch time, hungry and moody, in the heat of most mid-days.

The islanders were more about working with a paycheck attached to it. They wanted to take advantage of all the opportunities they had that their parents didn't. All educated adults I knew worked full time. They had an infrastructure of *Yiayades* (grandmothers) and retired grandfathers who were willing to pick up from school and run after their kids' afternoon activities.

Many of my contemporaries would leave from work and go to their parents, or in-laws, to find a hot meal ready for them, their children fed, and some, even with the homework done and extra-curricular activities covered for the afternoon.

It wasn't our case. I was playing the role of the *Yiayades* in my 40s, with a small George who needed lots of attention, and Rose and Diego as young children finding their way back into this land that was foreign to them. After all, they were so little when we took them away to the other side of the world, that they only remembered their school days in Sydney.

With all the implications of managing a household of five and attending the needs of 3 small children, people here would still refer to the fact that I wasn't enrolled in a formal job. Some asked: 'So how are you spending your time at home?', 'Don't you get bored?', 'Are you going back to teaching?' and even 'I'm sure you can do something online, working from home.' <eyes rolled up>

From Academia to Home manager

If you're a compliant, hard working, peaceful, 'soft' type of person, most probably you'll find the real world a nasty place.

Let me explain: Compliant, hard working, peaceful, soft characters in children are usually the ones rewarded at schools. They make the teacher's life easier and are good examples of the system 'working'. For those reaching a third or even fourth level of education, this translates into many years of "work hard, be good and get your reward".

In my case, some of the rewards were a scholarship for an international Summer camp, an educational loan for a Masters degree abroad and a full scholarship for a PhD in Mathematical modelling at a top European University.

When I left that student's world, there were many employment opportunities back in the mid 1990s. I got a teaching job and climbed up the academic and administrative ladder pretty quickly. I was fortunate to be in the right place at the right time. I enjoyed 10 years of success in education until I felt exhausted and took the opportunity to have a break from it all.

After the break, came my brief incursion in entrepreneurship, after which I realized that the real business world environment was not for me. I had been earning my income through, what I thought, was very hard work and some kind of external assessment already in place, for 15 years. It was pretty simple to me, as I was suited to it. It shouldn't have come as a surprise, then, that I found entrepreneurship utterly harsh and unrewarding.

To be a successful business person, you must have a natural ability to get what you want in unconventional ways - as every conventional way is already taken - and you have to feel pride in selling things.

The meaning of hard work when running your own business has nothing to do as with what is considered the same in academic life. While in Academia you are paid to focus on ONE particular problem, in Entrepreneurship you wear many hats and must impress as you wear them. That is why being the mother and the wife in a family is, in many ways, like entrepreneurship itself but without the income to measure its success.

Having grown up myself with a mother who brought up 3 successful and happy adults into this world, I knew that motherhood was a role to be respected at large. I had to get over the prejudice that in modern life we should all generate an income. I embraced my role as a home manager and family supporter and started to feel pride in the important role of 'being available'.

And at that point pre-menopause hit...

Pre-menopause and Hot flushes

It doesn't matter how much you read about this subject, if you don't live it, you don't believe it. Mood swings, sense of helplessness and depression, are just some of the natural events any woman goes through between her mid 40s and her late 50s. I suppose it's one of the most obvious ageing periods in a woman's life.

Once the years from when motherhood starts until you see your children fly the nest, are over, you are left with a sense of emptiness you never thought you'd hate so much.

I personally thought I'd be happiest once I was 'done' with raising my children, but I got caught in my ailing health. What I didn't know was that it was just the beginning of an irreversible process.

I didn't feel the hot flushes as much as I was aware of my mood swings. I blamed pre-menopause because I had never gone through that before. I would pass from feeling joyful one day to feeling miserable the next without any apparent reason. It did improve when I took a herbal extract that regulates female hormones and I stuck to it.

You're the youngest you'll ever be today

Thinking of ageing, I remember, in my mid 40s, how I learned to appreciate that photo I had just taken of myself. It always seemed not good enough until a few days had passed and I looked better in the photo than in the mirror!

If you are in your 50s, you've already lived many years. Children will see you as an old person and yet, I can see you for who you really are. There's no young or old in you, just wiser or healthier. We are who we are forever. Every day we wake up breathing is truly a gift. But it doesn't always feel that way.

I learned that how you feel and how you look are two different things. I don't think anyone in my age group, who didn't make it to this decade, would believe how much I can 'write' by just looking at me right now. Yet, today, I'm better than I will be in a week's time, and the same goes for you!

There was a point when I didn't recognise the person in the mirror anymore. It was like there was one me who never changed and she had to come to terms with the image in the mirror. For many years, until my early 40s, I always saw Clara in the mirror, but after I turned 50, there was an uglier person, sometimes resembling Clara but never as pleasant as I used to remember her.

I had Alexis to share this ageing process with. One day I asked him: "Do you sometimes not recognise yourself in the mirror?" and he said: "Yes, ob-viously!" in a tone resembling Alan Rickman's interpretation of Snape in the Harry Potter films. He used to make me laugh so much, I had loved him since the day he approached me with his lovely smile and said "Hi". It was a privilege to grow older with him by my side.

Every time I'd complain about looking old, he would say to me: "I'm looking old too, so we're in this together." That used to make me feel so much better and opened a path to deeper and honest conversations on the subject. I even dared to ask him one day: "Do you like this new version of you?" and he'd just casually say: "Sometimes I do and sometimes I don't." That would be a reason for me to relax and sleep in peace. We truly were in this together.

My parents were also fortunate to have each other whilst they became older. Only a loved one who can relate to how you feel, can comfort you when you reach that stage. If you only have younger people around you, they'll try and reason with you: "You are fortunate to have reached this age, mum, your friend X didn't make it this far." Well, yes, that's true but sometimes you need a little empathy from someone who can relate. That's all.

It's all relative

When I was 45 I didn't think my story would interest anyone. Now I know it can help some by immersing themselves into a different life experience, and perhaps, help them make better choices.

You see, it's all relative: Happiness, success and their counter-parts, sadness and failure.

You'll always be better off than many and worse than others. If you're reading this or listening to the audio book, you're already fortunate to be able to comprehend language and translate it into feelings and images in your mind. There is always someone less fortunate than you, to whom the simple things you take for granted would give enormous joy.

It is also important to know that it is Ok to feel miserable, even when your reasoning is telling you that you have everything to feel over the moon. We have our days, we are composed of so much water in our cells, and water is affected by the Moon. So we are affected by the Moon, the planets, the stars, the constellations and the people around us. Can we control all this? No way!

I always found it better to admit that I was in a bad mood. I stopped hating myself for feeling that way to start with, and it made me feel so much better. I understood when my children were not in their best frame of mind and I gave them space. Sometimes a hug was in order. Each person needs a different kind of empathy. Even showing empathy sometimes can backfire. They might just prefer to be ignored.

It is an art to be able to work out what each child needs at a particular time. I was fortunate to have the energy to really think about certain moments, to analyse the tone of their voice, their moves and actions. And like any other parent, I made mistakes.

I made mistakes while trying to avoid what I hated most from my own parents, who were doing exactly the same thing. I remember my mum telling me that if I thought she was strict, I should have seen my grandfather. And so it goes, each generation of parents avoids mistakes from the previous one and will make new ones for their children to avoid when their time comes.

Grateful for science

If I would have been born in the middle ages, I wouldn't have made it to adulthood. As a child, I had too many biological limitations that were not treatable those days and that would have made me, at least, a social outcast.

I was very short sighted, allergic and had a retroverted womb! These conditions were treated, respectively, by laser surgery, bioresonance or just the knowledge that sperms swim at 45 degrees North-West, so I just had to lie on my belly, after sex, to fall pregnant. Without knowledge I would have been almost blind, always sick and infertile. I've always felt grateful for science's progress.

Even today, I would have been isolated with my thoughts, unable to express them, if I didn't have the MRW machine. We are living in a time of unprecedented advances in science and technology that can care for our physical bodies. I hope it will always keep improving…

Rose

"How's my yummy mummy today?"

"I've been thinking in my solitude and you'll probably get a few more pages you might want to edit today."

"Looking forward to that, Clara. You look good! Did Georgie pass by today?"

"Yeah, at some point. I lose track of time. I only know when it's time for a long sleep or just a nap. Other than that, I'm just thinking and my mind wanders a lot. I hope my thoughts are not too dispersed."

"I'll have a look and will rearrange bits and pieces, if needed. And, on the time issue, what is time anyway, mum? What matters is that we can read your thoughts. I feel really blessed to live in this time and space. Am I the daughter of 'Clara the Wave' or what?"

"Ha! I was just thinking along those same lines. I love how much we are connected. Your mind genes must be all from me, even though in many ways you are like your dad. <wink>"

"How did you do that wink thingy?"

"Sunday inserted a new command in the MRW's program so that if I think 'emoji' it will open the '<>' brackets for me to include a facial expression."

"Cool!! You can go back to 'emojing' us now. Let's fill your feeder with some fresh shake. I just got a fresh lot of gorgeous fruits and veggies."

"Oh, how I'd like to chew a juicy steak right now!"

"I'll spray some essence on your palate. It's the best I can do."

"I can sleep and dream I'm chewing, then. Thank you, darling. I'm grateful for you and for my sense of smell." <hands together in gratitude>

Mistrust and acceptance

When I was in my early teens, and attending secondary school, I was a very good student. I was brought up to be like that and I never rebelled. Since I was compliant, I thrived as a pupil, when much of the knowledge just had to be memorised and, the few subjects that developed logic and analysis, had to do with numbers.

As a child, I remember the many times I changed schools as we moved from one area of the country to another. I needed to prove myself as a good student in every new school. I had completed my primary education across 4 towns in 2 countries with two different languages. My dad, Jorge Luis, was a nomad in search for better job opportunities. He even took us with him abroad to get an international qualification to continue his professional development.

My last change of school was after my second year of secondary. I dedicated myself to scoring top marks since I wanted to be able to choose any career that appealed to me at University. When the first term ended I had made it to the top of the 'Honour Board' where they used to place our photo next to the term's average mark. I gained some new 'friends' after that.

I was weary of making new friends since I was tired of losing them every time we moved at my father's will. I wasn't in much of a sociable mood by the time I was finishing secondary. I immersed myself in music lessons after school and I filled the rest of my time preparing for tests and writing assignments.

In this last school, we were given revision handouts for every Maths test we had. I was on top of solving the problems as soon as I got the chance, so I could juggle my music lessons while doing well at school. Most kids would wait until the previous afternoon to revise. Not me, especially if I had a busy afternoon at the music school. That was something I wasn't willing to give up for any test. I loved the environment at the music school, both as a pupil and as a member of the orchestra.

During the second term, I started noticing that, the day before the test, my Maths revision handout would mysteriously disappear from my pile of books. After it happened once, twice, thrice, it was no coincidence anymore.

I safely assumed, based on the evidence, that someone was stealing my revision handout the day before each test! Was it maybe hoping that I wouldn't do so well? I still don't know and it doesn't really matter. But after this, and after having spent the Spring holidays summarising a whole book for a Literature assignment only to have it plagiarised by another group, I learned to give up my intellectual ownership and never trusted anyone again.

This was one of the perils of growing up in a society in which cheating was way too common. It was a way of life for many people and families, to the point where they lost awareness of what was the proper way to do things and what was dishonest. It was sad to see how, even when a person didn't need to cheat to get a certain, desired, outcome they would still bend the rules purely out of habit.

I suppose it was because of this generalised behaviour that you had the other extreme, the very strict and correct way of living life, like the one my grandparents instilled in my parents. We were a family exempt from the norm, so we disregarded the generalised dishonest behaviours we would observe in our neighbours, members of our extended family and other people in our immediate social circle, to be able to connect with them on a personal level. They wouldn't be the people we would marry, but we had to accept the way they decided to live their day to day lives.

With time, I learned to appreciate the classmates who were with me those 3 final years in secondary, during my early teens. There is something about friends you make at that age that bonds you in a very special way. They know you for who you are, not for that important position you might hold that is supposed to be reserved for very important people. I knew them inside out. I knew who lied, who worked hard, who was supportive of others. There's no time like your teens when it comes to getting to know other people.

If you have the chance to stay in touch, you're even able to see how they develop into adults, some into parents, business people or successful professionals. Even if I didn't have the willingness to become attached to my school mates, it was a rewarding experience to meet some of them in person, after almost 30 years, in Australia, of all places. In other cases, social media allowed us to follow each other's virtual lives and that was also special.

Mum, tell me more….

"Mum, how come you got so empowered from all this envy around you?"

"I was, in a way, resilient, my dear Rose. My own mother went through a lot of bullying as she was the youngest girl of 9 children. She was pretty and clever, so she also felt the bitterness of envy around her. Your grandmother taught me how to use the Angels and our Mother in heaven. I learned to visualise myself covered in a cape of love, in different colours. These are simple empowering techniques, that are now taught at primary schools, but that didn't exist then, except from our own ancient traditions."

"*Abuelita* (Grandma) was a wise woman indeed, so ahead of her time by staying true to her traditions. And poor you, all those towns, just for primary. It must have been really hard."

"I suppose I have nomad genes myself. I do remember crying when it was time to say goodbye to the school, the neighbourhood or the home. But I knew it was for the better and I would quickly be ready and looking forward to a new adventure. It is not for everyone, though. You remember how difficult it was for you when we came back from Australia, don't you?"

"Oh, yeah! I'm still traumatised. I'm glad it was only one big move. I couldn't have coped with 4 different towns for primary!"

"And it was more than 4 schools, but that's not important. I suppose that, once you pass a certain threshold, you start to lose count."

"Why would you change schools in the same town?"

"Since you ask, I went to a school run by nuns for one year to prepare for the Catholic First Communion. That made it 2 schools over a period of 3 years in one city. It was an interesting experience though. I learned I'd rather attend co-educational schools after that."

"You're amazing at looking at the bright side of things. Seriously, your ability to adapt to this island's life coming from a tropical paradise had to do with all the training *Abuelito* (Granddad) put you through. You must thank him for that."

"Always, I am grateful for every experience in my life. If anything would have happened differently, the outcome I so cherish today wouldn't have happened. My parents were just the messengers of what the greater God had in store for me. That's my belief. You know I don't discuss much my own spirituality because of The Wave. Deep beliefs and convictions are never popular and, in a world led by compassion, you must be inclusive rather than exclusive."

"Yes, mum. You're right. You've done a great job in raising 3 children who are so different. Diego is so obsessed with theology you can call him a monk, I'm the science freak and George is the official agnostic."

"Thank you Rose. I appreciate your words of acknowledgement. Parenting is a real challenge and teaching spirituality to your own children is not something you can do once they pass the tender age of 8. I never wanted to impose a belief or a life rule or to sound judgemental to any of you. Especially, not after I had been brought up a Catholic myself. Instead of playing the spiritual guide, I prayed and still pray for each one of you. It personally helped me keep my fear of being a bad mother under control."

"Speaking of fear, I read about your fear of dying and how you didn't realise it was affecting you. When exactly did you realise that you were living in fear?"

"Four years after leaving Australia's good vibration and after 3 years of living in our island's despair and stillness."

Fear is harmful

There's nothing worse than living in fear. Regardless of your surroundings, fear will only go against your wellbeing. Having too much time to think can fuel fear and allow it to take over your life. The problem is, you don't always notice…

I feared for my life every time I was going to give birth, but after surviving each delivery and holding the baby in my arms, the fear was gone. There were the usual reminders about death during occasional funerals that didn't really make me aware of my own fear of dying. I only had the standard concerns about my general health and used to carry out the annual checkup at the gynecologist. That was about it.

Cancer, however, was a big worry for me since my late teens. The odds were for dying once the 'C' disease was diagnosed. I lost dear friends to it, younger and older than myself, and that fed my 'Cancer-phobia', as my dear doctor P called it once. He told me "Yes, there is 'C' and there is also 'C-phobia', an equally dangerous disease." This was in response to me asking to check for cancer markers in my blood 'just because'. We did check and my fear receded for a few more years.

In 2015 I took control of my fears. The first step was to identify them: I was afraid of cancer (again!) and death. I had lost a dear friend to cancer the year before and never took my life for granted again. The death of a young mother of four allowed me to feel grateful for every breath I was taking but also bugged me unstoppably until I admitted I was afraid to die. Once I admitted it, I felt immediate relief. This fear had been present and unidentified for so long that it produced harmful chemicals, in my brain cells, that aggravated my immune system.

Nicole

"Hola *suegrita*. Buenos días."

This is Nicole, Sunday's mother. She's the only one who calls me '*suegrita*', a Spanish version of 'mother-in-law'. My Diego attracted her with his Latin ways. They've been together since their early 20s and I love her as if she's one of my own children.

"*Buenos días Nicole. ¿Cómo estás hoy?* (Good morning Nicole. How are you today?)"
"I'm fine Clara, *¿Y tú?* (And you?)"
"Still thinking, smelling and seeing. And grateful for being able to do all three."
"Gratitude is such a wonderful tool, able to make all well for us. I've been feeling so much better from my flushes now that my frequencies have been optimised. I can't imagine how difficult it must have been for you without the wristband. I have my bad days but giving thanks always helps. How did you cope?"
"It wasn't easy at all. We just had to pay attention, practice our moments of stillness and follow through even when not in the mood. It was very difficult. I remember the garden helped and so did the walks by the sea, the moments in my piano room and the smile of a stranger on the street."

"I find I can enjoy doing some of the things I always did in the past. Resuming them is one of the most difficult steps."

"I remember how I constantly gave up piano, yoga, tennis and writing, yet I re-took them so many times. It eventually stabilises and you find your new self, older and wiser. Even without the wristband, we managed."

"Does that mean I'm going to feel 'normal' again?"

"You will learn what your new 'normal' will be. Like when you got used to being the mother of one. You accept your reality and you move on."

"Are you still moving on?"

"I am indeed! Thinking to you all is a real pleasure for me. This is my current life reward. I appreciate the time and interest you all show towards my thoughts. I am also feeling better prepared for my next trip to join Alexis and my parents once I'm done with sharing my memories. How's your new book coming along?"

"I'm half way through. I'll come and read it to you, once I finish editing, for you to think to me about it. Your thoughts are always appreciated."

"And you do me great honour by reading to me before you read to anyone else. <smiley>"

"Great to see you can emoji us again. Sunday told me about it. Diego sends his love. He's still in London. I'll join him tomorrow. Do you want another colour set for your ceiling device?"

"A new colour set is always inspiring, yes, please. Thank you, Nicole *mou*."

"You're welcome, *suegrita*. Sunday will keep us informed about you. Keep thinking. We love you!"

"I love you too!! Have a safe trip and give my love to my boy."

Music

I developed a habit in my teen years that lasted until my mid 20s: Every study day would start with piano practice, even though I wasn't studying only music. Apparently, I was one of the few people with both sides of the brain equally developed. It was such a tough decision to choose between science and music, that I carried on with both for as long as I could.

Music was my friend, my ally and the way to organise my thoughts. I later realised it is a way to quieten the mind so that new ideas can flow. Playing a musical instrument makes you live in the present moment because you concentrate on the sounds and your brain is stimulated.

Music is a way to meditate and to let the ideas sink, for problems to solve themselves. In the repetitions leading to the perfection of musical phrases, all feelings appear clearer in our mind and we become energised. It is a great way to start a productive day.

While I lived with my parents, I thought I was limited by the fact that my piano was next to the television set, so I had to stop practicing while the rest of the family watched their programs. When I had the chance to decide where to place the piano, I decided to build a small room with a door, in which I could isolate myself and play at whatever time I wanted. My plan couldn't have turned out further from the truth. Once I became a mother to George, he couldn't cope with the fact that mum had the right to isolate herself and make some 'noise'. Eventually he learned and I could finally enjoy my piano in my 50s!!

The Moon in a tri-lingual home

I always spoke to Diego, Rose and George in my mother tongue. One of my favourite topics when they were little was the Moon, *la Luna*, in Spanish. All three of them learned to appreciate the Moon in the evening sky. After some training, they were the ones reminding me of the beauty of our satellite shining against the dark sky.

It's a good thing to show your children how to appreciate beauty in nature's wonders. One day they'll remind you! As we grow into adulthood and get caught in daily chores and worries, it is the freshness of our children, while they're still young, that helps us cope and carry on.

Rose was more prone to getting excited about the Moon and the flowers. She'd say in perfect Spanish, when she was only five:

"*¡Mira mama, la Luna!* (Look mum, the Moon!)."

It was a reminder that I had been doing a good job. After all, teaching my children an extra language made a total of three for them, before even joining pre-school.

I knew I had to enjoy their early Spanish speaking stage for as long as it lasted. Once they went to school, they'd talk to me in whatever language they felt more comfortable using. Diego and Rose turned out English speakers since they spent their early primary years in Australia. George was my Greek boy. He started speaking on the island and picked up the local dialect as none of his siblings ever did. I used to call him *'mi grieguito'* (my little Greek boy) even though the local dialect is a rather distorted version of modern Greek.

Our small island turned out to be quite multicultural while my children were growing up. Speaking 3 languages in a family home wasn't so uncommon. It was the result of the first migration wave that started after the fall of the Berlin wall.

Migration waves: from crisis to love

There was a time when wars of all kind started to sprout around the world. After the cold war, the 'war on terror' and never ending conflicts in the middle East, there were rebellions against oppressors in Egypt and Syria, to name but two, that left many people homeless and hopeless.

Families eventually started to arrive in Europe. Just like the Cubans used to escape the oppression of the Castro brothers by throwing themselves to sea, on any floating device they could put their hands on, people from war torn areas, in Asia and Africa, started to throw themselves in the Mediterranean Sea to reach European shores.

Our island was on their way to freedom, so we did get to help families who were desperately seeking relief from years of horror in their homelands. Images of drowned children, floating on the shores of the Mediterranean, went viral on social media and made the tragedy so real to everyone, that a big movement of compassion and love gained momentum like never before.

The governments started to feel pressure from the citizens to do more, basically, to do their job properly.

Mainstream media was losing viewers due to negative news. People wanted to see more of the good in the world rather than always highlights of evil. Not everyone was aware of the effect of visualization and prioritization on what to spend our energy on, but the growing few who were, made the shift possible.

One thing I learned during those dynamic times is that big changes happen from a few brave people who are passionate about what they do and are convinced it is the only way. With a connection to Divinity and the right intention, all turbulent times end in a peaceful balance. It is up to us to decide what kind of peace we wish to achieve.

Political tycoons and dictators were defeated by little 'Davids', who would throw stones at them, as they prepared to fight against tanks. Corrupted politicians and unscrupulous business people, like Zinopoulos from Greece, would find their way to behind bars thanks to the moral values of the few, whose compliance they were unable to buy.

On our way to the victory of values over injustice, we had to face some opposition even from within our homes. It wasn't easy, for trendy teenagers, to accept practices of light that were not portrayed to their age group as the 'cool' thing to do.

George in 2025

"I cannot stand all those yogis forcing us to 'be mindful' at school. When Diego and Rose went to school they didn't have to do any of that."

"Times are changing, *Jorgito* ('little George' in Spanish). You will appreciate those techniques when you're older. What did they teach you today?"

"The 16 second ritual to calm down: breathe in 4, retain air in counting to 4, breathe out and hold your breath..."

"That's a good one. Now you know how to control yourself and not get in trouble with Mr. Andreou."

"Mm, hadn't thought of that. I might use it during German lessons. Good idea, mum. I'm off to my taekwondo training."

"Your beloved taekwondo is also a technique for mindfulness, I don't see what's so different about your lesson at school. I suppose it's because your class is the first one not forced to do religious studies but rather Mindfulness and Spirituality. It's just a more inclusive term, you know?"

"Ok, mum. Whatever. Bye!"

"Bye darling."

George was a challenging 15 year old, who lived in a world that was completely different from the one his siblings faced years earlier. It was clear, in 2025, that the way we grew up and prepared for our future, wasn't working anymore.

The sky was the limit, but it was easier said than done for a person my age. It was like evolving, in one decade, to what had taken 40, or even 50 years, for people in the previous generation to come to terms with. At times I felt like George was parenting me, instead of me him, and I decided to let it flow. Once fear disappeared, and I trusted that all would be fine, it actually was.

I wondered what profession my rebel boy would choose to pursue. Nothing like his dad's or mum's, that was for sure!

"Banksters"

The love of my life was a Banker. It was a profession many chose during his school days for its stability and potential career development in this part of the world. Little did they know it was going to fall so low!

It took many years for people to stop calling them 'banksters'. A few crooks had played the banking cards and shattered the reputation the profession had reached from ethical bankers, who did their job properly.

Once this irresponsible management of Banks spread to most financial institutions on the island, bankers became 'banksters' and they all fell prey to cruel generalisations and jokes that portrayed them as villains. I learned to feel sympathy for the spouses of politicians who have to cope with citizens always blaming them for everything. I also understood why they tend to socialise mostly amongst themselves. There was a point when I couldn't take another joke about the evil 'banksters'.

At the end of the day, discriminating against any type of profession is as bad as any prejudice. There are good people and bad people in any type of career (and we shouldn't even judge because who are we to decide what is right and what wrong?).

To me, as a Scientist, banking wasn't one of my career options but it wasn't an issue against marrying my prince. He was a wonderful person who taught me not to judge others. That was a big accomplishment for him, due to my speculative and condemning Roman Catholic upbringing. I only realised how judgemental I was when my husband would ask after a scathing remark I'd make:

"What do you know about such and such?"

Not being judgemental is one of the steps towards achieving the liberating virtue of compassion that makes the world spin. It's one of the teachings I owe to cultural differences between my native and adoptive lands.

Back to banksters, during the time we were in Australia offering banking (not 'bankster') services to the Greek community there, our little island was living the 'Zinopoulos fairy tale' that eventually led to disaster.

The Zinopoulos effect

It was like the story of the Pied Piper of Hamelin. Zinopoulos came, to what had been a Banking haven, and bought the loyalty of politicians, banking executives, wealthy business groups and the media. He drowned them in champagne and trapped them in his web of pure Greek charm.

Islanders can't beat continental Greeks when it comes to speech. What can you say when, for every word you know, they can enhance it with another twenty and you can't keep up? After a while you just put on the universal smile and nod as your brain melts in fatigue.

It was as easy for Zinopoulos and his peers to lure the islanders into their game, as it was for the piper of Hamelin to steal the children away from their parents. Intoxicated by the bubbly charm of their visitors, the naive islanders, who are hospitable by nature, danced to their tune and followed it, out of the safety of their well known territory, into a darker forest they couldn't navigate without the sound of Zinopoulos' pipe.

It took too long before the sensible messages voiced by a few brave heroes settled. They finally managed to kick Zinopoulos out of the island. When they analysed the magnitude of the damage he had done, it was too late to save the financial institution he had bled dry. Zinopoulos and his accomplices had sucked the life out of the best bank on the island.

Many years after Alexis had embarked in what seemed to be an honorable banking career, the total opposite perception for such a profession had festered. None of our children wanted to follow in their father's steps. Being a banker was completely out of the question for them.

After a couple of decades, life changed for the better and new career options were available to the younger generations. My own banker always said he would have preferred to do pure Physics or Engineering, if only he would have known better. A life in Academia and writing books, at an old age, were some of the dreams he didn't achieve as he got caught in, what he thought was, an erroneous career choice.

My Spartan

If Alexis would have chosen a different path, ours wouldn't have crossed and our children and grandchildren wouldn't exist. Alexis was always up for a challenge and he made the best of the role he had to play in fixing Zinopoulos' mess.

I assumed my role, as if I was the wife of an ancient Spartan, and I looked at Alexis as my own personal king Leonidas. I used to kiss the warrior goodbye every morning and I felt proud for doing, what we considered was, the right thing. I stayed away from any new acquaintances that wouldn't understand the battles we were fighting and made sure I started to raise my voice in defence of those who fought for a better island.

People went from blaming politicians to bankers and criticising all public employees, including teachers, as if they were all equally bad. This was unfair to say the least. Having lived in a country where politicians were more corrupt, I knew that things could be a lot worse and that not all politicians were bad, neither all bankers unethical nor all public employees careless.

Bubbles burst

While living in Australia, we used to visit the island once per year to stay in touch with family and friends. We could see the increased consumerism compared to when we left. This was happening as Zinopoulos played his pipe to those he wanted to lure. The effect seemed to have spread to all sectors of the economy. Was the government mimicking Zinopoulos?

All salaries were increased regardless of the profession, migration increased due to greater social benefits and hiring of labourers by the, no longer, hands-on business owners. Native waiters made way for foreigners and we had to order food in English, as the new faces in aprons, couldn't speak the local dialect. I started to feel like a stranger in my adoptive land.

I had already experienced a bubble bursting, in 1983, in my native oil producing country, Venezuela. There, a previous increase in oil prices led to over expenditure. Not investing in other economic activities, like farming and tourism, resulted in a financial crisis that involved devaluation of the local currency, inflation and unemployment.

I knew the warning signs all too well. It was just a matter of time for the pattern to, somehow, repeat itself in my adoptive land: Overspending would no longer be possible and many people would owe more than they could pay back.

One thing I learned from those bursting bubbles is that, those who remained grounded, never fell to the spell of the piper in turn. It was terrible to see how the government and banking institutions, on the island, leveraged themselves so completely on the Greek bonds. Not one banker raised a word of warning, it was more convenient just to enjoy the ride, and the luxury, in an era of apparent bonanza.

Sunday's back

"Good morning, *Yiaya*. Thinking of Zinopoulos, are we?"

"Oh, well. I´m hoping that enough people will read my thoughts. We have to warn them. Remember that after Zinopoulos came Rufini and then Martell, all causing devastation for those who fell to their spell."

"'Fell to their spell'... you love the sound of that, don't you?"

"<wink>"

"And *Pappou* is king Leonidas. Love that!! He did, after all, help in putting Zinopoulos behind bars."

"And I, Gorgo, the queen! <wink>"

"That makes me a princess then! Love it! Please think to me about another of your favourite topics: The rise of Rafael Ruiz after Taluro fell. I'm looking forward to the reception at Rafael Jose's and my friend Aleena's home in December. I need some insight for small talk, please *Yiaya 'Clarita linda'* (pretty little Clara)."

"Ok, let's change country and move to the stories from the other side of the Atlantic."

The Rise of Rafael Ruiz

In 2015, my birth country had been undergoing a 'revolution' for 17 years. A group of Latin American leaders had decided, at the end of the 20th century, to use Socialism as a populist ideology. They promised justice for all in a rich continent with far too much poverty. It was the so called 'Socialism of the 21st Century'. The truth was, they were following the failed model of the Soviet Union, adapted to Spanish speaking America by two ailing brothers, who ruled a nearby island in the Caribbean.

Hugo Chavez was elected President of Venezuela for the first time in 1998. He remained in power for 15 years until his early death in 2013. How did he manage to remain in power for so long? In a nutshell, Chavez spoke to the resentment of the less fortunate, he fuelled hatred between social classes in a country that had followed this structure, since its foundation, in 1810.

He convinced them to vote for a change in the Constitution and eventually approved Presidential re-election by decree. His argument was that he needed time in order to 'make it right' for those less fortunate. The people trusted him to carry out his vision of a better country, full of possibilities for all social classes.

I had left Venezuela before Chavez won his first election. In the many years I had been away, a new generation of politicians emerged. They were of a kind I never experienced while growing up: They were from more fortunate social classes than Chavez, of higher intellect and charm than any of the previous political leaders I knew, and with an incredible determination to not give up on their country. The latter was missing in most of us who had left to, what we considered were, better places to build a life.

One of these politicians was the great great grand nephew of our own Libertador Simon Bolivar. His name was Rafael Ruiz and he was a tad younger than me. He survived prison during Chavez' successor's period and became the first President of the new and prosperous Venezuela, in 2017. It is an event I have always cherished and I still get goose bumps when I think of his inaugural speech as President.

And our island was finally united

My adopted land was also a suffering nation for a lot longer than my birth country. Here, it had been fuelling of hatred forever. The local dialect is a mixture of Venetian, Turkish, Arabic and mostly Greek. It's a sample of the history of domination and struggle the islanders had endured over centuries.

A few years after falling prey to the European financial bailing in 2013, the time was ripe for solving a division problem that had started over 40 years earlier. People were tired of betting on the so called West. They decided to use what they had and make the best of it. The leaders of the two 'sides' of the island were born in the same town: beautiful Turnassol. They had the guts to sit down and make some tough decisions that were criticised at the time, but they eventually led to happiness and prosperity for the younger generations.

It was complicated to explain to my children, when they were little, why their father had to go to the army on regular basis. The island had an occupying army in the North 33% of its territory. Thousands had lost their properties, and dreams, in their seized hometowns, during a war that peaked in 1974. Since then, all the men had to attend the military service after finishing school, for 2 years, and then participate in regular activities until they turned 60.

I wanted to teach compassion to my children, and we were at the heart of the conflict's solution, but the fact that their dad wore an army uniform and attended regular activities, led my five year old George to voice the concern that there were 'bad' people that *Papa* had to defend us from. When confronted with the specific question: 'Are there really bad guys out there?' I had to give the best answer I could. A 'no' would have beaten the idea of his dad going to 'defend' us, so I said, 'They are on the other side and they aren't attacking us right now. *Papa* just has to show up so they don't harm us in any way.' This was the best I could do after 40 years of status quo.

Fortunately, the division had ended by the time George finished school and he only went for a 6 month peace-keeping training exercise. It took much work from all sides to finally solve the problem. Leaders had to overcome selfish interests, and focus on forgiveness and determination to join forces with those they had once lived with, in peace.

Sometimes, all it takes is the willingness to change. Just as people are placed in opposing sides by outer forces, they can decide to live together again, in peace, when the outside forces are not acting anymore. It seems humans act by inertia most of the time, until they realise they can decide on their own path.

Back to Venezuela

In 2024, I finally managed to go back to my birth country with my 3 children, with ages spanning from 14 to 25. We knew it was probably going to be the last trip as a family of five. It was a real pleasure to be able to visit my ailing aunts, uncles and some of my 55 first cousins.

Diego asked a million questions and practised his rudimentary Spanish. Rose decided to use me as a translator, and George used mostly sign language and a few swear words in accordance with his teenage vocabulary. Alexis and I focused on the aunts and uncles we had met during our trips in 1997, 2000 and 2004.

It was incredible that we had to wait 20 years to be able to return. And we were fortunate enough to experience a new paradise that truly portrayed what Venezuela deserved. After hitting rock bottom, people were forced to unite in an unprecedented way and the whole nation shone a new light of love, hope and compassion.

Small talk at Rafael Jose's home

Dear Sunday this is for you:

Eduardo Tentoza

Your great grandfather, Jorge Luis, after whom your uncle George was named, worked with Rafael Jose's maternal great grandfather, Eduardo Tentoza. They were both in love with the art and science of food production. They respected plants for what they really are: our source of Oxygen and the first level in food chains.

My own mother never forgot the day they all had lunch together and Mr Tentoza tore the paper napkin in two and said:

"It's a pity to waste a whole napkin considering all the trees needed to make them. Half a napkin is all we need."

This was probably the first statement about environmental awareness I had ever heard.

Rafael Ruiz Gil

Another story is that, when I applied for an educational loan to study abroad, Rafael Jose's grandfather, Rafael Ruiz Gil, was the president of the lending institution. (You will have to memorise all these names as the double surname is a very Spanish feature and it's the only differentiator between fathers and sons - remember your friend's dad is Rafael Ruiz Tentoza).

I did well on the exam and got the loan. You can use this as a memory of the good old times your *Abuela* (*Yiaya*) is still grateful for. How else would I have met your *Pappou* Alexis and had your dad?

Sunday asks another question

"You've helped me a lot for RJ's party, *Yiaya*, thank you. Give me some general insights about our cultural differences. I don't want to sound brutally blunt, as I seem to understand that they're quite sensitive even to the tone of your voice?"

"Yes, Sunday, that's a tough one and one I'm glad I didn't have to live with since the day I left. I'm afraid there are still remains of those codes of conduct inherited from the times when the country leader, in the late 1800s, admired French royalty."

"So, if I'm just the Sunday you know, will I be in trouble?"

"You won't be in trouble, especially since you're European. You're not assessed in the same way as locals are. You'll be fine as your own beautiful self, me thinks."

"Still I don't want to appear rude. Do I just add a general phrase to everything I ask like 'Forgive my bluntness but I'd like to know… or I think…'?"

"Yes, that's safe. In Spanish you can say: *'Disculpe el atrevimiento, pero...'* I'm sure you'll work it out."

"That's great *Yiaya*, thanks! I've been practising my Spanish online with interactive recordings from Venezuela so I get used to their accent and expressions."

"I'm sure you'll be fine and you'll enjoy breathing in the air some of your genes will recognise as theirs."

"I'm looking forward to nourishing my Venezuelan bits so much."

Women coming together: From Caracas to Sydney

Maybe women come together to realise that one is better than the others: better off, better looking or better loved?

Thinking to Sunday about cultural differences brings memories of my behavior with fellow women.

I remember my cousin Laura, who went to an all girl school, and how she used to categorise them as 'nerds' or 'wantons'. I didn't even understand the terms the first time I heard them. The 'nerds' were the introverts, or those who took studying too seriously. The rest would fall into the latter category.

I felt it wasn't that simple but it seems that there were issues, in all girl schools, that we never raised in co-education. We had other topics to discuss, as we stood in all-girl clusters, at my co-ed school. If I had to choose between being 'nerd' or 'wanton', I would obviously fall into the 'nerd' category.

I hated wearing skirts and felt more comfortable in trousers during playtime. Since I wore spectacles from the age of 5, I never saw myself as a girly girl. I used to find it simpler to communicate with boys than with girls, so I stuck to them. Certain questions some girls came up with used to catch me completely off guard.

As an adult, I remember meeting a family of 3 daughters in Sydney and one of the young ladies asked, in a playful way that reminded me of the style of my cousin Laura's all girl school:

"What's your favourite lipstick brand?"

It caught me so much by surprise that a professional young woman would present such a question. I didn't know what to say and couldn't even remember what brands of lipstick I used. It wasn't an issue to me!

I grew up with many more interests beside beauty products and, so, I wasn't acquainted with what many of my fellow girls were talking about. I suppose they trusted me as little as I trusted them. Maybe we just didn't know much about each other and that led to an invisible barrier. Ignorance can really separate fellow humans from each other.

Until my mid 30s, I didn't have the chance to belong in any woman's group. My friends were usually 50% from each gender until I was adopted by the most loving bunch of ladies I ever met. In spite of being 20 years older than me, they were very active physically and mentally, and supported each other during difficult times. I was far away from home and they invited me to join their Monday tennis sessions. They were the best Monday mornings in my life for as long as they lasted. There was no competition, no jealousy but pure friendship and support.

Such cathartic meetings, amongst women, are a true blessing and something to treasure forever in your spirit. To this day, while many of them are gone from this dimension, when I relive the pleasure of their company, I feel whole.

Ralph

Ralph is Rose's only son. He was conceived via IVF, from a donor's sperm, after Rose decided she wasn't going to wait any longer for the right man to join her in her quest to motherhood. She was already 38 and becoming a mother became a priority.

In 2040 the fallacy of postponing parenting had already been debunked. People were returning to basics and the biological clock was put ahead of some stereotyped life plan for success. Who said you have to travel the world before having children? Having children at the fertility peak, in your 20s, allows any woman to travel in her early 40s, with or without a family of her own, without dealing with babies at that age.

People who wanted to incur into parenthood early, and were mature enough, weren't put off anymore. I remember I was ready to form a family in my mid 20s, but the pressure to tick off a list of material goods and expensive experiences before we could embark into married life, didn't encourage any candidate partner to join me in my quest. I had to wait almost 10 years until I found my 'Greek Prince' ready to join me.

It was different for Rose than for most in her generation. She was pregnant at 40, like many of us in generation X. She had travelled the world alone in search of her true calling. It wasn't about postponing having a family, it was about beating her odds of developing colon cancer, like her *Yiaya* did, 10 years before she was even born. In Rose's case, there was no pressure for her to avoid motherhood in her 20s. It just didn't happen.

Like me, Rose was fascinated by Genetics and music from a young age and, with our support, she dedicated her life to use music as a tool to switch on the good genes while making the bad genes dormant.

One innovation led to another, and the years passed for her, without a break to settle down. She was a nomad, like her grandfather Jorge Luis, always in search for the best possible institution to support her quest to beating the cancer odds.

Once she settled down in a position that would enable her to carry out long term research, in one place, she decided to become a mother. Ralph has been a true gift to our family. He's like a younger brother to his cousin Sunday and a big brother to George's twins.

Rose is back for more work

"Hi mum. Mmm, you're thinking heaps about the family."

"Family IS life, Rosie dear. Would you like me to think about something else?"

"You should go back to politics in Europe and Latin America and how we ended up where we are today. There's a gap in your thoughts, so far, that would be interesting to fill from your point of view. Not everyone experienced modern history for as long as you did."

"It's all about living by Gandhi's words: 'Be the change you want to see in the world'."

"Think about how that actually happened, what a big impact it had on our planet and how we have evolved to where we are today."

"Ok dear, but I'm sure I'll drift back to philosophising about life and family."

"That's fine mum, you're doing great. I'll give you some dark chocolate today to fuel inspiration."

"Oh, yeah baby! Muse from Cadbury, courtesy of Rose."

Lipras and the domino effect

After the traditional ruling political parties failed to manage the European loans that were given to countries like Greece, Spain and Italy, there were a series of electoral victories from extreme left parties.

Lipras rose in Greece and Pablo in Spain. They failed to deliver what their populistic rhetoric promised and, before long, people understood that, even if the idea of a saviour Estate or Leader sounded great, it wasn't going to solve their problems. It cost Greece the humiliation of a lifetime and it spread quickly to other Southern European countries.

Rome and Athens saw their least glorious days in the mid to late 2010s. They rose again with more innovations than ever in the 2030s. Madrid took a bit longer to recover, but they also managed. All three countries are now part of the new Europe, together with our own united island, Ireland and good old France, Germany and the UK. Other countries decided to leave the Union and form their own agreements without the control of their North-Western counterparts.

The domino effect toward disaster in southern Europe, paradoxically, led to a quick recovery through wealth creation and innovation. Countries that were not trusted with being able to keep up with the development of their more organised partners from the North, managed to find the best in their peoples and both, lenders and borrowers, came out winners.

Many conflicts were solved in the early 2020s, because country leaders found common ground instead of focusing on differences. They realised they could benefit from what their partners would do differently to them.

The End of Populism

Gloria Álvarez is a political scientist from Central America, who started an educational movement, in 2015, about options to replace the failing populism. Her aim was to empower people, using technology, so that they could stand on their own feet and feel proud to do so. As she used to put it, humans are all selfish and her personal gain, from preaching her ideology, was doing something to change her surroundings. She was fed up with living in a place where too many people felt sorry for themselves.

After five years of hosting a radio program, where she listened to victims of domestic violence and people with low self esteem, Gloria learnt that individuals had to take control of their own destiny. Someone had to show them how to do it. She took that responsibility.

The world had run out of money from lending without return. In backing populistic policies, humans had created a planet full of needy and dependant people.

The same cancer that led to Europe's fall, and eventual comeback, had depleted the wealth in many Latin American countries. I could see a common pattern in the events that were happening in both continents. It all came down to values. The style in the Old world and the New World were different, but human beings had become more interconnected than ever. All it took was for the truth to triumph in the New World, so that the movement could be adopted worldwide.

Decisive sum of small efforts

The bravery of a few leaders from different corners of our beautiful Earth, broadcasted widely and freely, via the internet, allowed a connection between humans that reversed the events that were holding them back. Regardless of culture, surroundings or income level, all humans were liberated from their dependence on a saviour state, which was preventing them from reaching their full potential.

After hitting rock bottom and feeling abandoned by their leaders, people started helping each other and connecting through a common source of abundance and light. Spirituality took off in many different ways. There wasn't a person who didn't acknowledge the presence of a perfectly calibrated force that was holding our Universe in harmony.

East and West stopped calling themselves that. Today we simply have time zones, with no particular starting point. It took me years to get used to the idea that China was not the 'far East' anymore. It must have been the same for those who didn't believe things could get better and that justice and good would prevail.

Many messengers spreading the same type of message to solve a problem most people had, was the perfect formula for creating an irreversible and very much needed victory of good over evil. This might have sounded simplistic or even utopian in the 2020s but it's the proven key for global change. Once values regained their status as the only possible ethical monitoring system, people from different backgrounds felt included and sat down on the negotiating table.

Eventually, the spirit of the uprising that had started in Egypt a few years earlier arrived on the American continent. We recovered our paradise countries from the paws of a beast created in the name of an ideology that had nothing to do with what it had become.

Sunday brings Patty

"Hi, *Yiaya*. Here's Patty, our new cat."

"She reminds me of our Aphrodite, the first cat we fed at home. How did you get her?"

"She was abandoned in a cardboard box at our neighbour's door with another 2 kittens from the same litter. We decided to adopt this one and the neighbour kept the other two, so they can conveniently play together in the gardens…"

"Perfect!"

Cats and the common good

I was raised without hairy pets. We had a parrot, a canary and a couple of tortoises in the different homes where we lived with our parents. My mum was scared of diseases transmitted by cats and I grew up afraid of dogs, after a neighbour's Labrador approached my 3 year old self in a friendly barking body that looked huge to me.

It took the patience of stray cats, who would not leave their dung around, and who would happily accept any food remains we'd give them, to make me enjoy stroking a cat's furry body in my late 40s.

They came into our lives when the planet was immersing itself into this level of goodness and light we're in today.

Caring for pets was part of the transformation in our souls.

Diego, finally!

"Hello mum! You're looking good today. I haven't seen you in such a long time."

This is my Diego, with his deep voice and his tall silhouette. I never stopped seeing him as my baby, even after having another 2 babies and so many years passing by.

"*Hola mi amor. ¿Cómo has estado? ¡Qué bueno verte!* (Hello my love. How've you been? It's so good to see you!)"

"It's so good to be on paradise island, *'la Isla de la Fantasía'* (Fantasy Island)."

"You know I've always said…"

"The best feeling when living on the island is leaving it and returning to it."

"You keep interrupting me, you sharp, clever boy, now even in my thoughts!"

"I'm a 56 year old 'boy' now, mum. Sunday told me she brought Patty. Nicky sends her love. <kiss>"

"Yes, two of my favourite girls. You're a lucky man indeed. Now it's three, with Patty <cat>"

"You did a good job, mum. You raised me well and kept me away from abusers."

"Ha! Funny you call them that. Yes, you grew up during a time of fight for equality that turned out to be discrimination in the other direction, in many cases. I had to protect my boys from being 'abused'. I knew Rose wouldn't have any problems. The weaker sex in my eyes was yours."

"You also did a great job in making separate roles a valid option again. I don't even know how people could live in the delusion that both members, in any kind of couple, could play breadwinner and homemaker. It's not possible, let alone fair."

"You're such a charmer. Even in my condition you fill me up with compliments and make me feel like I'm floating about. Thank you, my love."

"I thank YOU, mum. I'm going to have to leave you now. I'll see you again before we leave for London."

"Bye darling."

Mars and Venus collide

John Gray is a name I'll never forget. He wrote about how men and women are different. Most importantly to me, he explained why, when most professional women arrive home after a long day in a testosterone producing job, they're not ogling in front of a screen, to relax, like most men do.

Most women are engineered to feel pleasure from jobs that have to do with nesting. Things, like tidying up the home, produce the female hormone for pleasure, Oxytocin. It is as simple as that and this wasn't even mentioned in the biology classes, at school, as it is now.

Understanding how male and female physiologies work differently helps in choosing the life role that will develop your full potential. It does not impose a specific type of role for females to pursue but, rather, makes homemaking a valid option, with as much social recognition as any job.

People had been so obsessed with some types of discrimination that they would, lightly, approve of abuse in the opposite direction. In some heterosexual couples, men ended up doing all the housework just because they were men, when it should have been a shared responsibility, depending on time availability and abilities.

My fight was always to give people more choices and not to turn the tables in the name of equality. Extremes do not work neither for gender roles nor for social roles.

Social recognition and social classes

Social recognition is a necessary evil in our human psyche. We are wired to be social and we wilt when we are ignored. Here I am thinking still, not letting go, even after my body has suffered the consequences of poisoning, through the very water I was drinking. It's because of the acknowledgement I receive every time a member of my family visits: "Family is the fundamental cell of society" is one accurate definition I learned at school.

Society can bully us as much as it can empower us. The worst effect is when it places you in a ladder scheme where you are above some or many and below some or many. No matter whether you move across or along the system, you are somehow always squashed by its many different levels.

I was brought up to look at people's heart and intellect, regardless of the level they were placed on, while holding on tight to my own step on the ladder so I wouldn't be pushed further down. The only possible way was up and I learned to give myself permission to climb to the top of my own ladder, by working with my abilities and knowledge.

One of the things I treasure most from having lived on this island for most of my life, is the simplicity of the ladder here. Everyone feels they can be at the top of their own ladder, even if it is just a stool!

Rose is engaged!

"Hi mum. *Kalimeeera!* (Good morning in Greek)"

"*¡Rosita! ¡Buenos días! ¿Cómo está mi niña preciosa hoy?* (Little Rose, Good morning, How's my gorgeous girl today?)"

"I'm well, *mami*. (mummy) Beaming, actually."

"Shoot!!"

"Roy proposed last night, mum. I'm so happy!! I said yes, of course. We're going on a trip and we'll get married in the Caribbean. How's Bonaire for a change?"

"Bonaire is a paradise, great for diving. You'll love it! What did Ralph say?"

"I think he's more excited than I am. He'll join us in Bonaire and then he'll go to Venezuela, with Sunday, to see Aleena and RJ. We'll have so much to tell you when we're back."

"I'll be here, thinking of you, and the good times in my native Caribbean."

"I'm going to be editing what you've thought, so far, before the trip. We still have plenty of time. The trip is planned for November."

"Tell me more about the details after the Wedding. Where will you live? Are you moving?"

"No mum. We're basically living together at my place. Roy will invest in the renovations I've always wanted and we'll make a legal arrangement in regards to ownership of the place. Ralph wants to be adopted and

Roy wants a grown up son, so it'll work out beautifully, I think."

"I'm so happy for you, my baby. Roy is such a great man and Ralph will have that father he always wanted."

"Amen, Mum. Going back to your thoughts, once I edit them, I'll share them to get some feedback and see what the best course of action is. Think more about the Social ladder theme. I see you were thinking about social issues before I walked in today. I love your perspective on that one."

The Social Ladder

I hate the social ladder. Even if I'm at the top of my ladder, there will be taller ladders around me, showing me how low I am. I do not like to step on other people, to climb to a place where I'll be alone, or sought by members of other ladders, just because I'm at the top of one.

The problem is that the vertical structure of society involves stepping on others to be able to climb. Why do we have to do that? There is enough ground to fit us all in a horizontal structure instead.

I love our island because there are lots of stools and only few taller ladders. And still, the latter are quite rudimentary and dependent on the stools. That makes the stools powerful. I like my stool. It allows me to be real friends with people on top of other stools and discourages jealousy.

When I was in the ladder structure, in my native Latin American country, I was looked up to, and sometimes envied, by people who were in lower steps in other ladders. I always felt bad for those who were in lower steps in my own ladder yet there wasn't a way for me to change their position.

The feeling of being below other people was, as unlikable, as the notion of being above others. I remember going to the most prestigious club in Caracas, the CCC, for a Christmas dance. I got the dress, the accompanying gentleman and the '*kefi*' or party mood. There was a live performance by the most famous Latin band of the time.

It was interesting to see the faces that used to appear in the social section of the Sunday paper, right before me. They were humans just like me. I could see them moving, eating, drinking and I thought: "They go to the toilet just like I do!" It was an eye opener!

Clara Díaz, Clara Díaz....

"Díaz..., Díaz...<wondering expression>"

This is how the 3D colour versions of the faces I used to see in print, almost every weekend, reacted to my name when I was introduced to them. I was frozen by their facial expression, as if they were questioning what Díaz this was. I realised that they wanted me to describe the family tree for this particular surname, which didn't trigger a nice feeling in me. It was another one of those topics - like the lipstick brand - that was never an issue to me before.

I was who I was, I knew my parents and extended family, some further up or further down their own ladders. It was just the way it was. I didn't have to expose myself in front of a bunch of tall ladder tops, looking down at others, to make the reality even more obvious. I had felt bad, all my life, for the inequalities in society, especially for those below me, without looking down at them. Now that I was being looked down upon, I hated the ladders even more and I wanted to flee this country with great determination.

I also realised, that night, that even people in taller ladders than mine, would struggle to rub shoulders with those occupying top positions in taller ladders than theirs. It was pathetic to witness the fake smiles, jokes, small conversation and mentions of their last trip or investment. Just thinking about it makes my stomach churn. <sick face>

Sunday in the Caribbean

"I'll be attending the Wedding and diving with Ralph in Bonaire, *Yiaya*. We will invite Aleena and Rafael José as well."

"I wonder if Bonaire is still how I remember it, the most untouched of the Dutch Antilles."

"I was reading about it and, yes, it's still the wildest of the three. Curacao and Aruba are the ones where the ship cruises go and where the largest Hotels were built."

"I remember a 7 course meal we had one New Year's Day in Bonaire. It was sublime!"

"But you were a regular in Aruba, weren't you?"

"Not as much a 'regular' but we did go 2-3 times, as a family of five, with my parents. It was so close to the Venezuelan mainland and you had a feeling of safety that would allow you to completely relax. Oh, the Netherlands Antilles and their '*Papiamento*' (name of their dialect). I loved those days. It was the most important investment your *Bisabuelo* (great-grandfather) ever made. He was a pioneer in investing in 'building memories'. Your great-uncle Tomas criticised him for not setting some money apart and saving in foreign currency, in an American bank, instead. My dad was too loyal to his country for that. We had tried holidaying within the country but the lack of security, even then, made us go to places where we could feel protected by the law. My father remained loyal to his country on everything else, never wanting to contribute to capital flight. He even accepted a few government positions, but found it impossible to cooperate with decision makers who were driven by politics instead of knowledge. He clung to Venezuela until old age, until the solitude of living so far away from all his 3 children forced him to take the decision he had been avoiding for 20 years: He left his beloved land and came to the island to live with us."

"Yes, my dad always speaks fondly of his *'abuelito'*. It's a shame I don't remember him, even though he did manage to hold me before he passed away. It must have been very hard for him living on the island after having a life in the country he so much loved."

A refugee of old age

My parents ended up living with us on the island. It was a tough but necessary decision. We were not able to visit them in my birth country during the final years of the 'revolution' and they were only getting older and more fragile.

Becoming a refugee is one of the saddest feelings I can relate to but not because I was one myself. I left my birth country voluntarily as a young adult. I experienced the 'refugee' feeling after being a mother and not being able to take my children, on holidays, to the school where I studied or to the beaches I used to visit as a child. In theory, I could, but the dangers I would put my family into were so high, that the sensible thing to do was to stay away.

I can only imagine how much more difficult it was for my own father. He had gained a reputation as a soil scientist and was respected and admired across Venezuela. He then left his friends, siblings and the land where he had grown crops, on which he experimented to improve their yield, during his professional lifetime. He had written 16 books, all in Spanish. He had so much to offer, still, and he had to leave in his early 70s.

I suppose it became too much of a burden to continue living in Venezuela: My parents were like prisoners in a flat for two. My father would have to wake up at 4:30 am to be on the road before 6 am, after he had a shave, his breakfast and the morning visit to the toilet. In a country where you weren't guaranteed clean facilities on the road, you had to eat and remove waste before hitting the road. The large intestines of all members of my parents' nuclear family were trained to empty as soon as we woke up. We also learned to carry filtered water and a snack with us.

As time passed by, for my dad, carrying out this morning ritual took longer and longer. He had to add some stretching and a basic work out to his routine. He used to do all of this very quietly, for years, as my mother slept. As they got older, she became a night owl and couldn't sleep for more than 4 consecutive hours without some herbal help to knock her off.

My father had won many battles in remaining my mum's hero as a breadwinner. At some point he felt the heavy burden of solitude at old age, in a place that no longer offered health care, medicines or basic foods, let alone personal security. He then decided to give up and come to his daughter and son in law who had always invited them to retire on Paradise Island.

Exile turned blessing

Growing older in a country where you don't know the language is tough. Getting older and not being able to control what you eat and where you go, away from your friends and other children is not the ideal situation. It was the price my father, Jorge Luis, had to pay to be able to see, at least, one set of grandchildren grow.

My mother, who was ready to become part of a larger family, enjoyed every minute of it. My parents became my children's 'Abuelitos'. They all enjoyed their roles, so much, that it was worth being a part of it.

At the beginning, I was afraid of how we'd all get along and how much of a burden I'd carry on my shoulders. My fear was a consequence of my body's weakening, due to chronic inflammation, from food intolerances. I couldn't physically cope with the idea of adopting a pet or adding another extracurricular activity to my children's schedule, let alone taking care of my ageing parents.

Once I recovered my strength, before my parents came to live here for good, I was able to see things clearly. It was going to be a pleasure to have them with us on permanent basis.

I knew that I had to show my own children compassion towards these two beings that had given their best to bring me into this world and to offer what made me who I am. I understood that I was also going to age and would be dependent on my own children. It was simply going to be easier for them if they saw me lovingly and patiently caring for my own parents.

This had not been in my original life project, probably because my parents never got the chance to experience caring for their own parents. My maternal grandmother had died suddenly before my mother got married and my grandfather followed shortly after, when I was only a baby. My paternal grandparents lived far away from us and we didn't see them on a day-to-day basis, so my father never dealt directly with his ailing parents either.

Once my parents left Venezuela, we had to find a way to provide for the lack of friends for them, as it is important to have a group of nourishing friends when you're older. The great news was that, being far from their children and grandchildren for so long, had made them technologically savvy and they used all this knowledge to stay in touch with their life-long friends and family.

In the end, the voluntary exile turned out to be more of a blessing for all. My children had physically present, rather than virtual, grandparents for many years and we had the privilege to see them move into the next dimension. It was my honour to be able to hold their hand when they took their last breath, only 2 months apart. They were a loving couple who left this world almost in unison.

Explaining Venezuela

It took one good looking and confident Gloria and her teachings on continental history and politics, for me to be able to answer a question such as: 'How come in a country with so many resources, riches and natural beauties there is so much poverty?' This was a question that came up many times when people heard my parents' story.

I grew up, like most people in my generation, apathetic towards politics and history. I was like the great majority who wanted to have a better life, through carving out a successful career, away from politics.

The word 'politics' had an offensive connotation as there were many who had benefited from belonging to certain political parties. They climbed their own ladders, as Union leaders or populist candidates, in elections they'd easily win at local or national levels, since there wasn't much competition.

Climbing ladders through politics became a way to create other 'exclusive' clubs similar to the most traditional CCC. Eventually the 'nouveau rich' started mingling and joining forces with traditional rich families. The elites multiplied and expanded, and so did the inequalities, the poverty and the resentment.

For those of us who didn't benefit from political positions, the rule was to not get involved, including not voting at all. We thought we should leave politics to the politicians, as if it didn't have anything to do with our daily lives. We learned our lesson and paid dearly for our misconception.

As for learning our own history, I always found the Ancient Greeks more interesting than our own civil wars and the power struggle, of the few, in our baby nation. It was probably my genes in action once more. It wasn't until many years after leaving school, that I understood how history explains everything in society. We must always be informed.

Gloria Álvarez preached all over Latin America that young people had to read books about history and political ideologies, and choose one. Knowledge was and is power.

Awareness and Polarisation

There was a point in the late 2010s when social uprisings didn't surprise us anymore. There were so many injustices in the world and they could be broadcasted for what they really were. People would simply take a photo or a video and share it on social media for the world to see. Blog articles would follow these images and, suddenly, there were millions of amateur journalists reporting from all the corners of the planet.

Mass communication enabled people to follow those whose message most resonated with them. There were public debates as comment threads on social media posts. It was sad to see how evidently polarised societies were.

There were referenda imposed on the citizens by irresponsible governments and you could see the exchange of insults between followers of a Yes or a No vote.

It happened in my birth country, many times, as the populistic Chavez government worked on changing the laws so they could take control of all powers and institutions that ruled the Nation. It happened in my adoptive land with attempts to re-unite the island, and it happened in other European countries as their 'unpayable debts' became more unsustainable. Citizens had to reply to questions like 'Do you agree with our country accepting the terms of the lenders for a new loan?' A way to avoid accountability, if you ask me!

A sad example of how it took to the Arts

One example of polarisation reflected in the arts is how two very talented, internationally renowned musicians from my birth country, reacted in opposite ways to events that many of us, Venezuelan born, were following on social media since 2014.

The indoctrination of the 'revolution' in Venezuela led to a counter-indoctrination. Some leaders of the 'new opposition' reminded us of the heroes who had created the Republic we grew up in. There were 2 opposite poles in the Venezuelan society of 2014: the Chavistas and the Opposition.

Gabriela Montero was a very successful piano soloist and improviser who wrote music about the loss of the country she knew. Many of us identified with her music and her messages. I remember the last time I visited during revolution years, I felt like I had lost the country where I grew up, exactly like Gabriela portrayed in her piece Ex-Patria. She used to take every opportunity to inform the public about the violation of human rights that was taking place in Venezuela.

On the other hand, the famous *'Sistema'* of youth orchestras had produced a very talented and awarded conductor who never said anything about his country shaped by the revolution. Gabriela never stopped pointing out how he was conducting a concert for an official celebration while demonstrators were being killed on the streets, not very far from where he was. When asked about his position regarding the government of Venezuela, his reply was that he was a musician and not a politician.

Just like these 2 musicians had opposite approaches to politics and bitterness grew between them, we sadly saw the same effect within families. Siblings stopped talking to each other, as mistrust prevailed, in a country where betrayal was rewarded by the populistic regime.

At the beginning of the end for the 'revolution', we all belonged to groups that wouldn't tolerate one another. We had to learn to forgive and find common ground so that we could all rebuild the country that we had lost to hatred and extremism.

Apathy became Passion

In 2014, there were a series of events that determined the beginning of the rise of the counter-revolution. These events led to the fall of the regime 3 years later.

People went from apathetic to following the day to day events with passion. Many, like me, were following even from far away. I admired the bravery of those raising their dissident voice in a National Assembly dominated by Chavistas.

I caught up with events that I had chosen to ignore all those previous years while living abroad, making a life in a foreign land. I became acquainted with those who had fallen in clashes with the national forces.

At some point, there were hundreds of thousands demonstrating in the streets, asking for freedom and security.

What led to this tipping point? One strategy populistic regimes use to remain in power is to make delinquents their allies. This allows them to infuse fear in the population and to remain free of charge for offences committed by ordinary crime. The drawback is that criminals cannot be controlled when set loose.

2014 started with the murder of a beauty queen who was very charismatic and a great actress too. The Miss Venezuela pageant was a yearly event we all grew up looking forward to watch. It was broadcasted by one of the main television channels in the country and we all learned to love the hosts, the choreography and the dresses. Beauty and baseball were two of the country's big entertainment industries.

Beautiful Monica had been elected queen in 2004 and was killed 10 years later at the peak of a successful and promising artistic career. She was touring the country with her partner and their young daughter. In between beautiful images that she was sharing on Instagram, they were attacked by a gang of young armed criminals who called their holiday short. Monica and her partner were both shot in their own car, with their very young daughter as a witness, as they were driving from one site to another.

This was a horrible event that didn't pass unnoticed. Many public figures condemned the level of violence that had been reached in the country. The authorities' liability was pointed out as similar acts had been spreading far too quickly amongst the less famous population. It was the start of a very tragic and decisive year for Venezuela.

The sad murder of Monica and her partner created a momentum for the opposition forces to get organised and mobilise people out of the comfort of their homes. Until then, the majority of the people wouldn't get involved into politics more than it was required. Maybe they'd call their regime-sympathising cousin to get an identity document issued swiftly, or they would simply carry on with their chosen life routines. Until 2014, most people were living in what they themselves called a parallel universe.

I personally cried, mourned and created a Twitter account just to follow the events from the island. Following Monica's death, massive anti-government demonstrations took place and terrible events unfolded.

I taught my mother how to use Twitter so she could follow the news that the local media wouldn't show due to increasing repression and government control. The regime was slowly choking all newspapers and TV channels that would appear to side with the counter-revolutionary opposition, even if that meant just reporting the facts.

I was in despair as the ruthless killings and beatings were reported on social media and I wondered why it was affecting me so much since I had settled into a new adoptive land for almost 20 years. A clinical psychologist I connected with online, from Venezuela, explained how no one can ever detach from his or her birth country. 'It doesn't matter how many years you've lived abroad, when your birth country bleeds, you feel the pain', she said.

Realising I could be an adopted islander and that my birth country would always hurt me, I allowed this budding passion to blossom. It was the drive I needed to start learning about history and reading about politics, so that I could understand what was happening in Venezuela and the rest of Latin America.

One continent, one history

Gloria Álvarez played a key role in teaching those who, like me, had grown up ignoring our recent history and political ideologies.

She offered a clash course for free on social media and never tired of replying to both positive and negative comments on her posts' threads.

The explanation for the situation of Latin America turned out to be as follows:

1. The original inhabitants of Central and South America followed a structure of social classes.
2. Unlike the migrants who arrived in North America, colonisers didn't arrive in our new land to work for their families. They went there to take whatever they could from the locals, by force. Gloria explained that instead of creating wealth, they were transferring it.
3. This carried on for centuries and determined the mentality of most people living there, who were descendants from the less favoured social classes. The class system that had been in place since the times of the original inhabitants of the land remained in place, only changing those who were at the top with the new colonisers.

4. The masses were easily led by any person or system promising to solve their basic survival issues with the least possible effort. It seemed they had evolved to serve people at the top of their ladders without any hope of ever climbing up or having their own stools.

Susie, Ralph and the twins

"Hi, Clara. Ralph and the twins wanted to say hello."

"Well, hello there! Thanks for stopping by Susie, dear. How have you been?"

"I'm fine, mum. Babies are keeping me busy. We're on our way to the beach".

"Are you eating properly and spending 'me' time as you should? You're looking good, by the way."

"Thank you. Mainly yes, I have the toddler's mother wristband to remind me to take care of myself too. It helps a lot."

"Are Claire and Anthony out of milk yet?"

"Yes, we're doing the sheep yoghurt and goat kefir introduction and it's going quite well."

"Oh, good on you! That's so important. Hopefully their generation's lifespan will be the longest we've ever seen."

"Yes, they're expected to surpass your parents' record."

"At the end of the day what matters is that they can live a happy life."

"Yep, there's no happiness in illness."

"I know. I'm so glad you're all into the Wave. I couldn't make your father-in-law beat his grandfather's life span, but hopefully our grandchildren will."

"How are you *Yiaya?*" (asked Ralph, who had been on his phone, chatting. Now he stood in front of the MRW screen to read my thoughts).

"I'm as good as I can be, my dear Ralph. How are you coping with all the news and plans for the rest of the year?"

"I'm so happy those two are finally tying the knot and I officially get a father! Roy is the only father I've met and my mum is so happy. Also, I can't wait to scuba dive in Bonaire."

"That's fantastic, darling. I'm so happy to see you. Every time you come, you're a bit taller."

"Thanks *Yiaya*, my mum sends her love. I went to spend the afternoon with Aunt Susie and the twins. We're on our way to the beach and I'll let them bury me in the sand. We've gotta go now. Bye."

"Bye dear, bye Susie, thanks for bringing the babies for me to see them. What a pair of cuties they are! Have a wonderful time at the beach."

Happiness shows

"Hi mum."

"Hi Rose. You look lovely today. I saw Ralph yesterday, on their way to the beach. You look really pretty!"

"I am happy! Joy must be having an effect on me."

"It is indeed. You know that very well."

"Yes, it all feels great! I'm enjoying every step of the way to celebrating my Wedding. We're working on the invites so people can save the date. Have to book a hotel here for those who can't make it to Bonaire. It's all very exciting!"

"So happy for you. How are you coping with the editing of my thoughts and all this Wedding planning?"

"Listen, I'm going to enter your thoughts in a competition for women writers this week."

"Alright. I'll continue to think. What do you reckon I should focus on next?"

"Listen, mum, I don't know if it's because I'm your daughter but I find your thoughts fascinating. I think it's important to tell your story in a time where there are still people who hesitate to embrace the Wave. There are remains of the culture stating that pills cure and surgical removals heal. We have to use all our resources to clarify what the real causes of disease are and how people can adopt healthier routines. You should also think about how cultural differences make us change perspective and grow as human beings."

"Ok, dear, I'll start from there and then move on to the Wave's history for those who are still confused."

"Sounds like a plan, mum. I'll leave you to it after I refill your feeder with some tropical fruits I got you this morning."

"Thanks, darling. Love you!"

"Te amo, mami!" (I love you, mummy!)

Acceptance through love

When I left my country for Europe, I was expecting everything to be better. I had grown up with the prejudice that anything from a developed country was better than what we had in my birth country.

I found that there were many people from other 'developing' countries, like mine, gaining knowledge in the UK. Their intention was to return and help their countries grow and improve. I realized I didn't share that intention.

Deep in my heart, I wanted to be able to never return to that unstable country I had grown up in. When the first two years passed and I had completed my MSc, I felt it was not time for me to go back yet. Not only was I feeling like a fish in a pond, I had met people who appreciated me for precisely coming from the country where I was born! I needed more time to find my perfect fit regarding career and, even, life partner. I was open to many options.

I did everything I could to extend my stay as a student in the UK and, towards the end of my MSc, I met a very special man who seemed to 'truly love me'. I managed to get an Overseas Student Award that allowed me to pursue studies at the PhD level in beautiful St Andrews, Scotland. I spent 9 months there and, at the end, love won over research and another degree. I was ready to get married and start a family. I didn't hesitate to leave the oldest golf course in the world and marry my prince.

Once I moved to Paradise Island, I realised there were many things I liked and others that were better in my birth country. I accepted the disadvantages in the name of love. I was happy to be away from the Venezuelan prejudices and I didn't know the language well enough to understand the prejudices in my new adoptive land.

Through experience I learned that being different doesn't make you better or worse than anyone else. I had to eliminate from my mind the concept of nationality ladder. Being born in a developed country doesn't make a person better than anyone else. We are all humans and we share many of the same basic needs, both physical and spiritual. Some cultures are richer than others in covering those needs.

My native culture shared the principle of nourishment through family with my husband's culture. It was great to be able to enjoy what this new place had to offer: security, organisation, stability and job opportunities. The setbacks seemed like a low price to pay for all the benefits I was now receiving.

This was my personal experience and that of my foreigner friends who also had the ability to adapt to this land in the name of love. I was fortunate to find a couple of Latin friends who married islanders at the same time I did and we shared many of our experiences in adapting to our new country.

Diversity enriches

After many years of living on the island and seeing several migration waves hit our new homeland, we could acknowledge that foreign genes had contributed to create a more diverse generation in terms of looks and behaviours.

Working in a school allowed me to see how children of different ages were living in what seemed to be parallel eras. Just a few years could change their views in ways that had seemed possible only after one or two generations had passed. Our world was moving at a faster pace. Children were exposed to so much more and had more choices than we ever did.

One of the obvious changes was the diversification of career choices that now included many in the entertainment industry. We concluded, as teachers, that the best advice we could offer parents was to let their children follow their passion so they could excel and be able to succeed. We then realised this approach was incomplete, as we needed to add the real possibilities of success for each child in their chosen paths.

Other areas in high demand were health, wellness and options for developing our mind and spirit. People wanted to explore new options to treat the increasing number of chronic diseases. We all seemed to know someone who had lost the battle against one of these conditions.

Bioresonance is everyone's friend

The fact that we are 'beings of light' wasn't as easy to accept as the fact that we produce energy. Eventually the physicists ended up 'enlightening' us all. Even those scientists who couldn't stand the expression 'beings of light' in a metaphysical context couldn't deny that there are photons in our body cells, thus the light is indeed within us.

Bioresonance uses measurable energy travelling around our body to diagnose where there is a problem or what external factors lower that energy. Some machines are able to restore the frequencies that allow our organs to function at their optimum efficiency. Nowadays, these are portable devices like the pendant or the wristband that my children use but when I was introduced to them, the machines were huge and we had to pay for treatments in specialised health centres.

I was fortunately able to use bioresonance to balance pathological frequencies in my body from foods I didn't tolerate, except for those from the sea. I still remember how happy I felt when I found out there was a therapy that would allow me to eat some of those forbidden foods again. I wouldn't be the freak anymore when eating out or appear impolite by refusing a home-made cheese pie. Especially on this island where eating is the preferred way to socialise and food is the ultimate form of indulgence, I was happy to recover the ability to oblige.

Bioresonance was also an option to killing germs by lysing (destroying) them in their own frequency dance. It didn't take much to convince me of its effectiveness since I understood the process but it took a lot longer to convince the general public. How could they kill bacteria using waves? Wasn't that what antibiotics were for? Yes, it was and also the indiscriminate use of them had led to the development of the, so called, superbugs that were very difficult to kill.

We grew up going to doctors who would prescribe a medicine according to the symptoms we presented. It was the method of suppression of symptoms rather than eradication of the cause. This was all good for some conditions. When I went with my story of food intolerances, they'd just tell me to stop eating the foods for a few months and then try again.

Believe me, I did. It never worked with fish or anything from the sea. Bioresonance showed that I am intolerant to iodine. This is a rare inherited condition and so I really had to ban sea products from my diet.

I also discovered, with bioresonance, that I could eat freshwater fish. I could literally take any product I was dubious about and check the resistance of my body to it. After so many years of living in the dark, I finally started to see the light.

I was also diagnosed with Candida overgrowth, a nasty parasite that was living all over my body and could have even been perforating my gut and causing my avalanche of intolerances. Candida is present in 80% of women in its pathological form and it produces tens of toxins and varying symptoms. I eventually treated it with a naturopath's protocol and started feeling stronger and much better.

I became a believer in holistic medicine and a fan of bioresonance. I wanted to share my story with as many people as possible. The majority of patients were thinking in terms of fixing problems with chemicals rather than strengthening their body for it to heal itself. It was the time I coined my hashtag #QuestToWellbeing.

There's no magic pill to healing

The truth is, not even Bioresonance can heal on its own. I hope my grandchildren will grow up understanding that they treat their bodies to the chemicals they ingest 3 times a day or more, every time they eat. Now that we have learned that convenience can kill, people are putting more emphasis in looking at every step in the food production system, choosing healthy options and demanding the elimination of poisonous substances even if they affect only some members of the population.

I remember when I realised that wheat and soya were officially labelled as allergens, in bold letters, on food. At the same time, they were both still broadly used as food additives. I couldn't understand why they had to add wheat to soya sauce, but there wasn't time to answer all those questions, so I concentrated on researching the important ones.

We had to reinvent the way we were feeding ourselves by going back to basics. Only when people put pressure on the producers to really go clean on how they were growing the beings that were going to nourish us, did things start to change.

It took many years for people to start connecting the fact that it's through your food that you get ill or heal. There's no magic pill that will cure you. Medicines can help relief symptoms and are certainly valuable in helping our bodies recover from dangerous infections but we cannot become dependent on them. You just have to keep strong both physically and mentally and use your spirituality to keep you going until it's your time to leave from this dimension.

From individual to collective

Why did we all hear about the damaging power of microwaves and still exposed ourselves to them? It wasn't just the convenience of quickly warming up our food. Many other habits were wrong but still adopted by the majority of us. We needed harmless options, as practical as the ones we were used to, to replace bad old habits.

Eventually, as more of us gained awareness, a tipping point was reached and worldwide legislations were put in place to protect us from our lazy selves. They started the compulsory screen-free periods at fixed times in each country or state. The only way to achieve this was to switch off all the internet servers except for those needed for matters of National Security. Everything else could wait.

Brokers and workaholics thought they were going mad but they eventually turned to the gym or just got in touch with their surroundings. It turned out to be such a pleasant rule, that now it's applied at each working place's convenience without switching off the servers.

There was also the issue of the water quality. Much of the water we were consuming on the island was contaminated with heavy metals. Some people were more sensitive to it than others and many were unaware of the harm it had on their health.

There were systems of filtering and purification you could install in the homes, or small devices with powerful metal clearing power. But it wasn't until they installed them on the municipalities' water outlets that we started to see a receding trend of the cancer epidemic in younger people.

As our world became a healthier place, it also became a less hypocritical one. People stopped worrying so much about being politically correct and they started speaking their minds on social media. This led to public debates on all areas: health, politics and events that were happening all over the world. In exchanging views we learned to listen and to put ourselves in other people's shoes.

Social inequality was made more evident and more professionals became interested in finding the cause and the solution to the problem. We finally understood that we are all connected and that we truly have to help each other at different levels: First the basic needs of food and shelter must be covered, then self-confidence has to be restored and, finally, our surroundings must provide a secure ploughing ground for people to develop their full potential.

Only by empowering ourselves can we lift others up and be lifted by them in return. It's as simple as letting love take over any other negative feelings like jealousy or anxiety. There is enough wealth in this world for every single one of us to flourish. Just let it be. Every individual has the right to become interested in any cause according to their internal voice. We need them all, especially the ones with views completely opposite to our own.

Sunday comes to visit

"Hello *Yiaya*. Good morning. It seems you fell asleep over deep philosophy here."

"Good morning, *koukla* (greek word for doll). Your aunt Rose asked me to focus on two subjects and so I did. Is it too heavy?"

"The topics are difficult. You've done a great job summarising them. It would probably be a good point here to give examples of how you coped with social injustice. Was there anything you could do individually to help? Were there organisations you could get involved with?"

"Ok, I'll go back even further, while I was still living in unequal Venezuela."

Professional beggars

As I was growing up in my beautiful tropical paradise of contrasts, I was trained on how to 'deal' with the problem of poverty around us. In our family, we would help the poor(er) by giving them jobs in the house when we needed help. We even gave food to children who would explicitly ring the bell and ask for 'some help' meaning money or food.

It was clear to me that individual efforts would not solve the problem. My dad would always point out that the 'problem' was that if you gave food or money to everyone who rang the bell, they'll pass on the message and you would end up with a queue of beggars that would be impossible to cater for.

My mum would give them food most of the time: a tin of tuna and a pack of pasta that they could take home to help feed their family. As time passed by, little girls would grow into young women and then my mum would point out to them: "You've grown into a strong young woman, why don't you go and work instead of begging? You can do better than this." They would never come back after that.

It was difficult to keep a balance. You didn't want to abandon the ones who truly needed help but you couldn't distinguish them from the ones who took advantage of the situation. They even made a film while I was still a teenager on how some children were brought up to beg as a profession. This concept stayed with me for the rest of my life. In most cases in a country full of possibilities, begging was a choice.

Victim of the inequalities

During the years I lived in a country with an obvious social structure, I always felt the unfairness of the system. The feeling of wanting to help, and not knowing how, never left me. Neither did the feeling of protecting myself from the harm that could come from violent forms derived from the unequal distribution of wealth. I suppose I was wired to survive in a hostile and unjust environment.

This is how we grew up: 'avoid that neighbourhood', 'don't wear jewellery', 'be home before the sun sets'. The problem only grew worse during the years of the 'revolution' as common burglars were armed and empowered by the regime to coerce voters in their favour.

I got a taste of falling victim to delinquency only once: At 15, I was walking from the music school to the bus stop, when a couple of teenage boys, slightly older than me, were walking in the opposite direction. As soon as I was at arm reach one of them quickly stretched his hand towards my chest and I felt pain at the back of my neck. By the time I looked down at my chest and realised my pendant was gone, the 2 lads were running away. They must have thought I was going to scream or ask for help.

I just stayed put and mourned my golden pendant that had been a present, for my 15th birthday, from my Godmother. It was a calendar of the month I was born in, with a diamond on the date of my birthday. After that experience, I never wore visible jewellery again.

I was lucky because I didn't live in the capital Caracas. I was in a smaller city where the *modus operandi* was lagging behind. Some of my aunts, who lived and worked in Caracas, were forced to give their jewellery at gunpoint while on public transport.

No one ever went to the police, once your watch, chain, ring, earring or pendant was taken, it was gone forever. Burglary and street robbing were so common that the police couldn't cope. They were never able to trap the bad guys. It never ceased to impress me how efficient our island police was in comparison with what I remember from the Venezuelan police.

Many police officers, while I was still living in my birth country, grew up with the robbers. They were mostly of poor background as their salaries and benefits wouldn't set them on taller ladders.

Hatred led to love

It wasn't only in my birth country but in many other places around the world in which the unequal distribution of living standards started to affect everyone. Less fortunate people migrated to places where they could have a stool of their own.

The interconnection between countries that were far apart was becoming more obvious. It didn't matter if the peoples had been oppressed one, five or 10 centuries, they would all prefer to move to a place where they could offer a better future to their children. And it turned out it could be done without geographical displacements in some cases but with a simple change in mentality.

In the unfortunate case of Venezuela, social differences were used as the means to divide and conquer, with the implementation of the, now failed, socialism of the 21st century. In more developed countries, there were radical groups with messages of hate against less fortunate people. These groups of extremists grew more and more popular until almost everyone had a 'team' and felt very strongly about it.

Stronger reinforcements to hatred made the differences more obvious and more painful. When there are two teams battling to win, there are losses on both sides but, more importantly, there are many caught in the middle. It came to a point where people couldn't remember why they were fighting against someone and started to feel tired. It was then that the Wave started to gain momentum.

People realised that negative feelings were just harming their physical health and their relationships with their loved ones. It wasn't only siblings not talking to each other due to political differences. It started to be intergenerational at some point too. In other countries it was religious wars or civil clashes. It didn't really matter what type it was. There was a time when conflicts became unbearable and were affecting places and peoples who were miles away.

We needed to teach our children better. Those of us with small children could still influence them in a different way from what we were seeing in young adults in the mid 2010s. As we aged, some of us realised that we needed compassionate children to take care of us when the time came for us to leave this dimension. Not everyone leaves life suddenly and painlessly, some of us become dependent and we are still very much aware and alive.

What would I have done today if the MRW didn't exist? I would have drowned in my frustration and would have been long gone from this world. I personally started to cultivate my spirituality in a more conscientious way in 2015. I went back to praying with my younger children at night, with our hands palm in palm in front of our chest, like my husband's old picture from his childhood.

Global or personal?

You might be thinking, what does social struggle have to do with you praying with your children?

It is the understanding that we can make a difference by cultivating loving practices. Prayer is just one way of calming the mind and accepting that there is a source of abundant love and security to calm our fears and other negative feelings.

By simply putting your hand palms together in front of your chest, you're activating important energy centres in your body. Try it if you don't believe me and feel the warmth that fills your hands after only a few seconds. It is not by chance that this is a traditional posture for prayer in many different religions.

When two opposite social, political or even religious poles started to look at what they had in common rather than what made them different, they could work together for the better life they all wanted. If we didn't have love and forgiveness, we would have never been able to move forward. It was a matter of getting our priorities right. Was it more important to dwell in the bitter past or could we all work together for a better future?

In reciting simple prayers with my children, I reminded myself and taught them that we are all imperfect and we can trust a higher source and ask for an abundance of what we need to live a happy life. They used to love the notion of the Guardian Angel, just like I did when I was small. It's reassuring for kids to know that there are other loving forces they can cling to, even when mum and dad are not around.

In a broader context, prayer helps us realise that we are all responsible for the way our world develops. This is paramount in achieving global changes. As we carry out our duties with love and compassion, we allow the best in us and in others to flow. We lift each other up to better places.

There were also some amazing Church leaders who showed humbleness never seen before in their predecessors. We had the first Latin American Pope in the Catholic Church who spoke even to the atheists, saying that they could also go to Heaven. This inclusion was the kind of attitude that was needed at a global scale to make this a more compassionate world.

It took quite a rebellious Pope to get my attention again. I was relieved to have changed religion to one that seemed not to impose so many rules on my life. I was extremely disappointed as a teenager when the AIDS epidemic reached its peak in the late 80s and the Pope then insisted on the fact that using contraceptives was sinful, even if it was a way to prevent contracting HIV when having casual sex. Of course, according to him, there shouldn't be casual sex at all.

I've always thought that, regardless of what you believe, these are private matters that shouldn't be ruled by another person. I happily accepted the more open-ended ways of the Greek Orthodox Church. Not that any religion is perfect or offers an easy path but the approach to people at different stages of their spiritual maturity is important. Having a Church leader who talks about condoms being forbidden in a good Christian's path is not a very clever move for the popularity of the institution.

Remembering Alexis

"Hi *Yiaya*. You're doing so well with your thinking. How are you feeling?"

"<Happy face>"

"Have you always been an emoji person?"

"Oh, yes! I remember when my own mother used to message all of her 3 children as adults, we loved to express ourselves with emojis. I mean her and myself, as the boys were more of writers. And your *Pappou* Alexis was more of an emoji man when he used to text me. <hearts>"

"How did you know *Pappou* was 'the one'?"

"I suppose neither of us really knew until we split shortly after we met, forced by the circumstances: He had finished his course and went back home and I stayed in the UK writing up my dissertation. I don't know about him, but the emptiness I felt was unprecedented. I told myself I'd never have another man in my life. Something similar must have crossed his mind because, a few weeks after saying our rational goodbyes, I got a phone call from him asking me to 'still be together' and I got an official invitation to see him on the island. Bingo!!"

"I wish I can find true love like you and *Pappou* Alexis had or like my mum and dad."

"And so you will, dear. I remember your dad asking me how your *Pappou* and I met, when he was only 15. I did tell him that Alexis had reminded me of my cousin the first time I saw him. He looked familiar amongst a bunch of strangers in a community of international students. But how you meet is not the most important question. I think you've asked a more useful one: how do you 'know' who is 'the one'?"

Meeting the one

This is one of those topics that does not have a correct answer. Generalisations are inaccurate to say the least, as we are all unique in our needs. This is as true for love as it is for health.

Knowing who the right person to share your life with is, is as blurry as defining happiness or finding the perfect diet. Each person decides whether they're sharing their days with the right partner or not.

It all depends on what their looking for in a partner.

Do you want to procreate? Look for good traits.

Do you want a hands-on partner in parenthood? Make sure you see them in action with other people's children.

Do you want someone you can talk to? Test them for the right amount of listening and their way of responding.

Do you want someone to take care of your domestic affairs while you focus on something else? Make sure he or she is a hands-on home manager and will be willing to support you on your endeavours.

It is so important to define what you want a life partner for because you will overcome all the bumps once your main need is covered. One big plus makes many negatives disappear, so make sure you make a wish list and tick options. Test the waters and listen to your gut feeling!

The gut and feelings

It wasn't until 2015 that I heard the term gut microbiome. Scientists around the world were studying how different populations of bacteria and other microorganisms living in different parts of our body, affected important functions such as digestion, nutrient absorption and even mood and weight control.

Since our human cells are many times larger than microbe cells, we are made of 90% microbial cells and 10% human cells in numbers. Symbiotic microbes are not more than 1% of our body weight though.

It turns out neurochemicals produced by our brain cells affect the microbes living in our gut. The process works both ways: our brain is also affected by our microbiota. Some applications of these breakthroughs were that we could improve our thoughts to heal other parts of our body dependent on our microbiome or aid the good microbes to thrive to heal our mind, or work on both simultaneously!

Listening to your gut feeling is now a scientifically accepted life attitude: If something doesn't feel right, it's probably not benefiting your mind and soul, so run away from it or change it if you can.

George is back from Amsterdam

"Hi mum. *¿Cómo estás?* (How are you?)"

"Hi Georgie mou. So good to see you. I'm still here, thinking and happy that you came today. How was Amsterdam?"

"Oh! You'll LOVE what I have to tell you. There was all this talk about the Wave and how we should go back to basics. Go mum!!"

"Good to hear that. We've won many battles and hopefully your children won't have to experience the poisonous effects I have suffered and so many who left this world before their time."

"The new legislation they passed on food is in favour of organic and whole produce. The more natural, the better. But they also included a genetic map to help people recognise the types of food that better suit them. It's based on family trees and geography. Very interesting."

"And what did you find this time to introduce to the islanders?"

"There's a new pineapple that grows in our Mediterranean weather and can be grown alongside aloe. It's a combination that allows you to get the best of these two powerful plants. They're both drought resistant and reproduce by sprouting. A farmer's dream, really."

"Will you spray some of its essence in my palate to get a taste? I love pineapple."

"I will mum. I love you! I felt so proud. You can't imagine. I even felt inspired to start my journey inwards. I'll ask Sunday to lend me a wristband and see how it feels too!"

"Go George! Now, you've made ME so proud. I love you so much, my darling!"

It took time but it seems I'll see it in this lifetime

George is seemingly engulfed by the Wave. I'm so happy for him. I remember almost 30 years ago, when 30 years seemed like a very long time, how resentful he was that I had dedicated so much time to public speaking and to my own journey inwards.

I can't blame him. He was just a budding young man and he felt abandoned by his mother, in comparison to all the attention his siblings had received, according to his own perception as a child. He didn't realise that he got away with more than any of his siblings did, as both Alexis and I knew better than controlling him all the time.

His circumstances made him the successful entrepreneur he is today. If he would have gotten all the attention and help he craved, he would have just been another academic. Every family needs the money maker, the improviser who can adapt to changes and we are all very proud of George's accomplishments.

He divorced his Russian mistake, whom he met in his late 20s, and now their gorgeous looking daughter Irina is blossoming as a ballet dancer in Stuttgart. My long lost granddaughter. She's tall, thin and disciplined, a very talented, 14 year old, dancer. Her mother took her away from the island when she was only 7. They went to Moscow and there she was trained to join the Youth Ballet of Stuttgart, which she succeeded in joining 5 years later. George was devastated by this separation from Irina and concentrated on growing his groundbreaking business: a healthy food delivery system.

George met Susie while immersed in his quest to success and she was the soothing companion he needed to enjoy fatherhood again. They were blessed with twins, Claire and Anthony, only a couple of years ago and now he's talking about getting the wristband and looking inwards. Fantastic!

Rose is here again

"Good morning, mum."

"Good morning, love. How's my future bride?"

"I'm good yummy mummy. Wow! You've thought a lot and we're on the right track."

"Isn't this thinking printable idea coming to an end?"

"Mum, you still have so much more to share with us. Move on to your 60s and give us some hope for the future, just like Abuelita Pepita gave you."

"Well, my mum made it to 90 and she was in much better shape at 88 than I am today."

"Yes, mum. It's this generational disadvantage we have to clarify so that we can prevent it again when the time comes. We're already being helped so much by the Wave and the wristband. Water quality has also improved so much. Your example has helped other people. You've done a terrific job. We've developed so many ideas with your support and inspiration."

"Thank you, darling. And the MRW machine! Speaking of which - or shall I think, 'thinking of which' - have you heard of Diego and Nicole? When are they leaving again?"

"We had dinner last night at their place. Roy and I went to share the details of our Wedding plans. I'm sure they'll pass by to see you before they leave. I hadn't had the chance to talk to them before yesterday. Ralph started his football training and will start his new school year soon, so I've been aptly 'entertained'."

60 years young

After all that I went through until my late 40s, I never thought I'd feel so good again in my own body. Being healthy and strong at 60, was a dream come true. I had always admired my special Australian friends with whom I played tennis when they were 60 and I was 40. I wanted to be exactly like them. I didn't know if I could make it.

It was not only how the island's water damaged the hair and the skin, it was also damaging my gut. There was a silent internal wear taking place as my hair and skin lost their suppleness.

One thing I always bore in mind was that my time was limited. It made me want to put my discoveries out there. Mass celebrityhood helped me gain the confidence to start spreading the knowledge online. I was almost 50 then and I started organising meetings with my local followers. The interest grew as more and more people were suffering from similar problems to mine.

We knew something fundamental was making us sick but we couldn't find a cause. So we started by sharing the solutions we had found individually to each of our problems. I knew it was crucial to create a network of like-minded people as I was stepping into older adulthood. Even if I couldn't have my Australian friends back, I could at least replicate the effort they put into staying fit and supportive of each other.

Ten years later I was well known beyond the island shores and I very much enjoyed organising events that would attract followers and ambassadors of the Wave from all over the world. I wanted to give every health practitioner, every diet enthusiast, herbologist, writer, artist who offered a soothing option to chronic fatigue or guidance for general wellbeing, a chance to promote themselves or their product. Selflessness led to success and I felt comfortable in an area in which I could use my academic background and my passion for teaching.

Being 60 and healthy is one of the most pleasant rewards life can give anyone. For me, it was the time my children had flown the nest and I had regained my space and time to finally stand for something I believed in.

I was paid to talk!

Teaching and public speaking go hand in hand. What doesn't seem to concur is the willingness of people to pay for a talk than it is paying for a formal 1 hour lesson on any school subject.

The problem seems to be that, unless there is an external exam to sit at a given date and time, the accepted compensation for retrieval of knowledge seems to be 'company over coffee'. It has to be made crystal clear that 15 minutes of any type of specialised attention on any topic is worth a professional fee and not just an informal meeting.

Just like a woman pays her gynecologist for a 15 minute check up, you should be compensated when dedicating the same amount of time to someone else's issues on an area that you have grown to handle and manage successfully.

Since I had gone from teacher to failed consultant on social media marketing, I knew how to handle myself the third time round. I offered my services as a speaker and started sharing bits of my story only after being paid for a speech.

Those who felt identified accompanied me and told others about my talks. From wanting to create a solid group of like-minded people around me for the harder years of older adulthood, I went on to inspire thousands of younger people who were willing to pay to hear me talk and to get their questions answered.

I can only share my life experience, and we cannot extend a life whose fate is to end just by having positive thoughts or exercising or having a balanced diet. That is probably why I never wrote a book, I stopped blogging and every speech was different. I was more of a researcher and a devil's advocate than a person who stood behind one single project.

I eventually opened a place where I could meet people seeking conversation with me on private basis. I called my practice The Wave, after sea waves, radio waves and ripples of information. The Wave seemed to be the perfect name for what had become of my professional self. And eventually the ripples it made reached the most remote corners of the planet. It seemed that in this diverse world, there were people vibrating at the same (wave!) frequency who were able to synchronise with me.

I was happy to reconnect with my Spanish speaking world through my message and enjoyed talking in my native Spanish a few times per year. There were many places in what used to be the Western world where people identified with my story, a story of migration seeking a better life and of physical and psychological small challenges. Cultural background was not a differentiator. There was common ground in wanting the best for ourselves and for our children's future.

More about the Wave

It's very difficult to define the Wave. It is about being honest in regards to being happy, to being healthy and to having a more meaningful life. The truth is that there is no magic formula. The more I grew my network of like-minded people, the more we realised that what works for one person doesn't necessarily help another.

It also has to do with admitting to ourselves that, even when living under optimal conditions and aligning with the habits that most resonate with us, there will still be days when we aren't so enthusiastic or so sure about being happy. We can use some techniques to oxygenate our brain, to remove toxins from our body and soul, and still, feel miserable.

One of the greatest achievements of the Wave has been to provide a platform for people to be able to express their frustrations and feel that they are not judged but rather heard. Empathy is very important in reassuring people, during their low days, that it is ok to feel that way.

At times it felt like I was sharing information from opposite views. And, yes, I occasionally came across research results that seemed to be in conflict, but that was part of being objective. The fact that I wasn't being paid by any particular company producing food or remedies, gave me the freedom to report from a diverse group of sources.

Many times I debunked a myth about the goodness of a particular product or practice. I was always open to criticism and, with time, I learned that we are easily wired to accept things at the absolute level. We wanted to be told what was good and what was bad for us. In order to accept the simplicity of 2 different categories, we were willing to go from one to another with the same ease as we would accept what goes in each category.

People liked the simplicity of statements like 'running is good for you' or 'coconut oil is good for you'. Then you'd get the retractors: 'running can harm your knees' or 'coconut oil contains too much of the bad cholesterol'. The key was to practice and consume everything in moderation. A combination of different products in your diet and different exercise activities were the easiest and simplest life hacks, as they liked to call it those days.

An important part of the Wave is the spiritual experience and one I always left hanging in my presentations. I didn't want to put off those people who felt very strongly about being agnostics. Sometimes they were so swayed by commitment that if you 'dared' to even bring up the topic of spirituality in a discussion, you'd put them off. Having mothered George through his rebellious stages, I knew better. I wanted the Wave to be as inclusive as possible.

Spirituality is a personal experience and one that no one should impose on others. What works for you might not work for others or could even go against their wellbeing in some cases. But the trilogy of body, mind and spirit is an inseparable one that we must all nourish for optimal results.

I have been a mother, a daughter, a wife, a sister and a friend. All my insights are from my own particular experiences. Some will resonate more or less with others who have been through similar experiences. I have in no way assumed that I am anything like a healer, a psychologist, a philosopher, a spiritual guide, a dietician or a health practitioner of any sort. Clara Maria Diaz Rodriguez, *'para servirle'* (at your disposal), just a caring soul who likes to connect with others.

In comes Nicky

"*Hola suegrita. Buenos dias.* (Hello, mum. Good morning.) It's a beautiful day outside, can you smell the rain?"

"*Hola* Nicole. Yes, it's nice to be able to see the grey clouds this Autumn and to smell the *'tierra mojada'* (wet soil). It reminds me of that song my father used to sing. RIP my dear dad. Did you bring something for me to hear?"

"Yes, my own story. We're off in 2 days and I wanted to get some feedback from my new draft based on the Zinopoulos case."

"I'll be all ears. I can do some reading time. Thank you for sharing it with me. You know I love the topic."

"I think it's important for the younger generations to understand that reinforced accountability on all the levels that exist today is the product of years spent shifting our values in the right direction."

"Yes, dear, so true. I'm so glad you're writing in your unique style. I'm sure it will definitely grasp the attention of the new readers."

"I hope it will make children think about a world without the security we have today, so that they appreciate the legacy their grandparents worked for."

"I'm sure it will inspire me to continue thinking after I have completed the story of the beginning of the Wave.

It also reminds me how important our childhood lessons are. We grew up with stories of good policemen reinforcing the law. It was nice to be good. Suddenly it was all about being politically correct and not having stereotypes and the main ideas got lost in translation. I can't wait to hear your story."

Déjà vus

Why did a simple Biology lesson at 11 have such a great impact in my health at almost 50?

We cannot measure the effect our learning will have in our future lives. Most of the times we are not even aware of how much it influences our everyday life. That's why looking inwards is so important. In order to listen to our own voice, we must quieten our mind. Then our déjà vus will become clearer and we will be able to understand the root of our problems.

In 2020 there was a growing scientific community accepting that the body is connected to our mind and that spirituality is part of the healing process. There were so many skeptics swayed against the terms meditation, spirituality and couldn't even hear the words religion, beliefs and traditions! We just had to keep going and embrace them into the Wave as they grew spiritually still denying the use of the terms they so much rejected.

When George was little, I remember one day he specifically told me that he didn't want to grow up and become a father and then a grandfather because he didn't want to die. He was only five years old and already voicing out this fear that I didn't conquer until middle age. We had progressed over 2 generations. I was very proud.

Including topics about mindfulness in children's story books had become a way to introduce them to these concepts that their parents probably knew about but weren't sure as to how to introduce to their children.

Other issues like the importance of standing up for your values are also included in books like the one Nicole is writing. She's specifically tackling accountability. It is so important that the children today learn their modern history, which my generation was writing for the benefit of their own health.

Accountability

The common denominator of many problems we had in the mid to late 2010s was, that people who were in positions of power, deciding for the many, could get away with selfish resolutions.

A tipping point was reached after problems like migration and increasing health issues got out of hand. As people moved, even illegally, from less fortunate to more secure grounds, the problems weren't exclusive to certain areas or countries anymore. These problems became global issues.

Citizens, who expected their governments to care for their basic needs of health and security, realised that they were not alone in their frustration thanks to global communications. Victories from groups or individuals who advocated for their rights in different parts of the world were broadcasted on social media. They inspired more people to get organised and fight for change.

One brave voice raised above conformity, could now be heard beyond geographical and even language barriers, and reach those who needed to get the message. This was one good effect of polarisation brought about by mass communication. People with the same problems were looking for similar solutions and, with all the online possibilities they united and slowly started to feel more powerful.

Citizens started to realise that their governments, as administrators of each country's resources, had to be made accountable for how their good or bad management affected them.

On our island, most families were somehow related to a political leader, a public employee or a banker. They started to look at the reality as a product of their own mistakes. Everyone had to take responsibility for the decisions they had made.

My good is your good

It took some brave leaders to change the idea that common good was dependant on a Messiah. It is not popular to bluntly express that it is only hard work what moves societies forward. Eventually people understood that it is far more fulfilling to earn their own success than to owe it to another person or system.

People also started developing their spirituality to cover their non-material needs. Many of the leaders, who endured imprisonment or even torture by totalitarian regimes, were very spiritual and open about it. Trusting a force that was beyond our limited human comprehension seemed to give them the power to overcome what appeared unbeatable.

Rafael Ruiz, in my birth country, was a living example of what we can achieve when we stand up for what we believe. Other leaders in the less favoured European countries, forced to austerity measures by the richer lenders, were also a source of inspiration to their followers.

As many were stripped of their dreams and hopes of a better future, they moved into a spiritual path to be able to cope and to find strength to carry on. Not only did it work at the individual level, it spread to many different levels of society.

We had to stop looking at ourselves as separate entities and work for our neighbours', friends' and relatives' good as much as we did for our own. This was key, in re-uniting our wounded island, and for Europe to rise strong again.

Latin America was finally acting like our own Simón Bolívar had envisaged it 200 years earlier: A huge piece of land with peoples united by their language and their history. It was enriched by new immigrants from less fortunate countries in Asia and Africa, and it is still rising to the top of the world today.

Australia developed in a different way since it is so isolated geographically. If you haven't been there, you must live the experience. They were already ahead of the rest of the world since its foundation. They developed from the notion that they were all descendants of the convicts that arrived from Europe. After falling so low, the only possible way was up!

It started at the schools

Teaching our children about the way their body works helped them make use of the available tools for them to live a happy and fulfilled life. Once the educators understood the connection between brain, body and everyday habits, they could pass this knowledge to the younger generations.

Our children were taught basic principles like:
- Pleasure hormones are produced by happy thoughts.
- The definition of happy varies from person to person.
- You cannot feel on top of the world every single day and that's fine.
- Breathe and realise how fortunate you are for being able to do so.
- We are all wired differently, so the definition of happiness is personal too.

There were pop-ups and picture books about how different individuals found pleasure in doing different things. Children knew what yoga, meditation and prayer were, depending on how religious their parents were.

The career possibilities included more options than ever. Children wanted to become anything and their desires were all important. They stopped the negative bias against farming and working the land. People had to go back to basics or they would starve. We had to take control of how our food was being produced. And that is precisely what happened.

From and to the land

In 2015, the average age of the island's farm manager was 55. As unemployment continued to be relatively high, new careers had to be offered for those seeking alternatives that would lead to a better future.

Horticulture and animal farming were amongst the new choices, together with technical options for the oil extraction industry. We needed to feed ourselves and stay warm in the winter months.

I personally loved this change because I had learned to value the contact with the soil in my own home's garden. After having grown up with the idea that working the land wasn't 'cool', I had understood that every person needs to be in contact with mother Earth to feel rooted and grounded.

Splitting families

In my 70s, once the Wave had taken off, I was mature enough to talk about broken marriages to those going through such painful situation. I had experienced my own parents going through their mid-life crisis when I was 19 years old. I grew as a person whilst I went through counselling and trained for self-awareness.

It was due to a painful situation that I started my own personal growth experience. It normally is. If we live in an optimal environment, we normally have our ups and downs but we don't really question why we behave in certain ways. There has to be a shock for the majority of us to start questioning ourselves.

As I grew into my own mid-life stage, I was very aware of all the changes we were going through as a couple and as a family: We were getting older, less patient, less tolerant, suffered health drawbacks, dealt with teen children, faced inflation, financial crises, political mistakes in our countries, uncertainty, aches, ailing parents and much more.

I always had a plan in my mind as to what to do if hypothetical tragic situations would take place: Alexis dying, us divorcing. I felt grateful for every smile from my prince going grey, for every hug I was able to give him or my children. I started focusing on the positives reality presented rather than on the negatives my mind would drift towards.

I felt very sad when I heard of friends in their mid 40s or early 50s who separated. It made me stay on my toes and monitor my own home and relationships within my nuclear family. My mum, then in her mid 70s, would know what to say, how to read the signs. I watched and learned.

Eventually I turned 70 and started to support couples who were going through the painful situation of separating after 15 or 20 years of marriage. For whoever wanted to attempt reconciliation, I had my own mother's example to refer to. I knew it wasn't easy but I could always refer to my parents' story. They chose to be together after a turmoil that lasted over 2 years. There was a price to pay and they chose to pay it. It was a valid option.

I was always supportive of my women friends who decided to remain separated, as this would have been my hypothetical choice in case I would have gone through it. My Alexis was a great husband and we managed to have a loving relationship for over 55 years with no turmoil, a true blessing.

I knew there is a shift in the way divorced women are treated by their female friends who remain married. I used the moments when Alexis was away to meet my divorced girlfriends. It became easier as the children became more independent and needed less of my time.

Bye Diego and Nicole

"Good morning, mum. We're on our way to the airport and we wanted to give you a kiss before we leave. It's going to take a while for us to come back this time."

"Hi Diego and Nicole, *mis preciosos!* (my beauties!) What are you up to this time?"

"I'm doing a study with the colour ceiling device, mum. We need to reproduce the results we've got with you so that we can get enough evidence on how it can help people who are bed-bound."

"Statistics, repetitions, I know! <heart> And you have to go off to a place where the sample can be significant. Our island is too small."

"Yes, mum. And it will keep me there for a long time. Hopefully I'll be finished before Christmas."

"Nicky mou, how's that gorgeous story shaping up? I love how your child readers learn complex concepts through simple stories. You're like a modern Aesop, really."

"It's shaping up really well, the vision board you suggested has helped me a lot. I've got the illustrators working on some images. Zinopoulos character leaves jail as a new man and advocates for justice from those with fortune and power."

"I'm so happy I've lived to see all this evolution taking place. I don't know if I'll see you again, I'm feeling like going to Alexis soon. I miss him and he's been waiting for me for 3 years now. I will stamp my thoughts for you to do whatever you like and then, I'm in God's hands."

"Don't say that, *suegrita*. We'll only be gone a few months. You're doing so well, we would miss having you think to us. You must wait for Rose's wedding and Sunday's stories with the Ruiz family. Who's going to guide her in her South American adventures?"

"She's got my genes, dear, plus you're a latin lover too, so she'll be just fine. Alexis is the one feeling lonely. You know he's always been impatient. Even though he's enjoying his parents' and uncles' company, he wants to share all the fun with me too. And, as he says, share me with them!"

"You're thinking as if you see him every day, mum."

"I do, *Dieguito*, dear. Just because he's not visible doesn't mean we don't communicate."

"Mum, I love you, I always will and I'll have you in my heart every day whatever path you take or I take, like since the day I was born. You know the lights were just incredibly interesting in that nursery but I was fully present in your arms. And I've always been."

"I love you too, my gorgeous and special son and the lovely couple you and Nicole make. You go and be fabulous both of you. I will certainly have a better perspective from a different dimension. I know you won't feel bad for me. I've had a long and fulfilling life."

"Bye bye mum, big kiss."

"*Chao suegrita. Te amamos! Gracias por todo.* (Bye mother-in-law. We love you! Thanks for everything)"

"Don't get teary you two. It's only another trip and I'll be waiting 'in the room next door.'"

Cheers to YOU

I don't feel sad saying my goodbyes to my children. I know I'm going to move to the next stage soon. How different it feels today from how it felt 45 years ago! I can definitely say (or think!) that I've had a fortunate life. My cycle has been completed and I am ready to meet Alexis and finally chat with the spirit of my mother-in-law. I always wanted to have a conversation with her. I'm sure we have many things to talk about.

And how's my father-in-law doing, and my parents?

I can't wait to see them all again.

And my Australian girlfriends, now ageless. What a blessing!

I have enjoyed thinking to you and I want to thank you for having read so much. I don't know when the MRW machine will stop recording my thoughts, so I just want to dedicate a few lines to letting you know how much I appreciate YOU reading my story. I won't be around to meet you in this dimension so I want to express my gratitude from the bottom of my heart, while I can.

Thinking to you has been a blessing. It made me remember happy moments and times I shared with dear friends in my adolescence, with my own parents during my childhood, my brothers, cousins, and how serious problems we faced were sorted out. I have lived 88 years through very interesting times.

I would like to raise my glass to the next 88 years and congratulate you for living in a more loving planet. It is up to you and your communication with your God or however you prefer to call it. There is no other way. Live your life to the fullest and always ask yourself if you were going to die later today, would you be doing what you're doing right now? That pretty much puts things into the right perspective. That's why I greatly appreciate your time.

Sunday asks how Clara was in her 20s

"Hi *Yiaya*. My parents left, so you'll be seeing more of me these days. What have you been thinking here? What's this about meeting with the dead? You're not ready to go yet, you can hear me, see me, smell me and I still NEED you here for some more time. I want to know about you when you were my age."

"I'm still here Sunday, going nowhere today. I'll think to you all you want for as long as I can. Saying goodbye or thank you is not a death sentence. I was giving your dad and his siblings, advice on how to live in case I was gone since my mid 40s, and here I am, almost 45 years later, still thinking and communicating. This is another myth that has to be debunked. Living each day as our last helps us put things into perspective, don't be afraid to talk about death and your feelings about it, dear."

"I know, *Yiaya*, I'm just biased when it comes to the idea of losing you. Only now I'm mature enough to appreciate your wisdom. I was living my selfish life until very recently and I want to know so much more about you and how you overcame all the challenges life presented you as a young adult."

"Alright, my darling. I was very much like you when I was your age. Don't be hard on yourself. You are going to be fine: happy and safe."

"Amen *Yiaya*, I hope so. Tell me about yourself at age 20."

My energetic 20s

I wasn't patient at all in my 20s. I grew up demanding a lot from myself and everyone around me. I was always involved in too many educational activities with no time for recreation. I never planned for games or social gatherings, unless it was my birthday!

This pattern of filling time with learning activities remained with me until life made me slow down. It couldn't always be about using time in a 'useful' way. I later learned that recreation is fundamental for a happy life.

It wasn't until I came to live in this village, in my late 20s, that I started developing tolerance towards the quieter and slower pace of life.

To toot or not to toot

I remember the day I tooted the horn at an old man in a van. It turned out he was 'the' bread man of the village and I later saw him 'everywhere': In the shops, at Church or just out and about in the village. I realised my husband knew him. The embarrassment remained with me forever.

I had grown up in a city with the population equivalent to that of the whole of this island. Life moved at a faster pace in a noisy city, where traffic demanded tooting the horn to remind the car in front that we had to get somewhere as quickly as possible. The anonymity I was used to there was not the case here.

I had to adapt and learn to patiently wait for the bread man to double-park, provided he had left enough room for cars to barely pass. I had to force my female brain to accept that there was enough room for my car to go through. And it did.

Years later, in my late 40s, I could see that same impatience and fast paced lifestyle in other young women who had just started driving and possibly earning their first salaries. I could relate to what they were feeling, that sense of accomplishment and freedom that is followed by the need to procreate, sometimes.

Underestimating simple house chores

Another side of my young adulthood was my arrogant attitude towards women who felt pleasure in the simple tasks of housekeeping. I remember when I was able to decipher bits and pieces of conversations between older women in the village. I was astonished to discover that they revolved around the way they chose the colour of the pegs while hanging the laundry, or recipes. I hated recipes. And I paid for it.

"*Yiaya*, I'm sorry to interrupt but I can't believe what I'm reading here. You??"

"Yes, Sunday. Me! I was my own worst enemy to reach fulfillment in my role as a home manager. I didn't know anything about nesting instincts or the pleasure of Oxytocin production. I thought a testosterone producing job, that would pay for others to do everyday tasks for me, would prevent me from ending up like the elder women of the village, talking about mundane chores."

"You really did change a lot since your youth. No wonder you were such a great advocate for giving home management the value it truly deserves in society."

"Yes, darling. Can you believe that when I eventually became a mother and was exhausted from doing it all, we were forced to bring a full time housekeeper and I was JEALOUS of her staying in my home while I was going to earn money to pay her?"

"Yes, I bet that's the way we ought to feel. I haven't experienced it myself, but at least I was taught that staying home is one of the possible occupations for women who are fulfilled by performing nesting tasks."

"Well, I didn't have a clue about any of this then. Years later, when I understood what I was cut out for, I enjoyed choosing pegs by their colours and your aunt Rose noticed! That day I understood that there are priceless moments between mother and daughter that can only take place in the quietness of enjoying simple tasks."

"That's a statement worth of your social media tag #QuestToWellbeing."

"It probably was sent on my social accounts when I was promoting The Wave."

Neuroscience explains a lot

As I moved into my 30s, and I was developing as a teacher of young adults, I remember interacting with the students the same way I had with my own teachers and parents.

This is a technique that doesn't always work, as each generation develops its own ways. I remember once I got caught up in an unnecessary argument with one of my teenage pupils, as I took offence at the blank look he gave me in response to a query I had made to him.

Years later, as a mother, I read Tricky Kids by Andrew Fuller, a clinical psychologist who explained how the frontal lobe of the brain rewires during teenage years. He specifically referred to the 'blank looks' that teens give their parents (or teachers) and how they are not pretending not to understand what you're telling them. Some teens simply cannot understand why we get so upset over issues they don't consider important.

Once I understood that they were not pretending, I could tolerate their 'blank looks' better. This was a lesson that went beyond teenagers and allowed me to question all those times when I was impatient or intolerant towards other people's behaviours. There must have been neurological reasons for them to act the way they were acting. I started to become more tolerant in general. You've got to love science!

Lifting others up was the answer

As I became more tolerant towards others, many changes were taking place in the world. People realised that the Robin Hood approach of taking from those who had more to give to those who had less was not fair. It would eventually lead to everyone becoming poor, unmotivated and dependant on the State.

Revealing the truth about Communism using technology was simple. One photo showing those who got to power in the name of this ideology, living the life of luxury they so much criticised when they were candidates, was very saying of how hypocritical most of the populist leaders were.

The ideology that had failed in the former Soviet Union, whose rhetoric continued to be used as election tool, also failed in the rest of the world. No one who had worked hard to afford a certain lifestyle was willing to give their goods to others. When it was their turn to have property confiscated, they all agreed it made more sense to empower those who still waited for their Robin Hood.

This new approach of lifting everyone up, while protecting individual efforts, was effective: it motivated people to stand on their own feet. It's what Gloria Álvarez called Libertarianism but not only this.

Compassion and tolerance had to be included in the equation or the efforts would be lost in discussions and definitions. You couldn't make a communist become a libertarian, so we had to look at basic values of justice and opportunities for all and make people from all political backgrounds feel included.

Tolerance and forgiveness

Making mistakes and feeling bad about them is the only way to develop tolerance towards others. For as long as I remained a perfectionist and was so demanding with myself, I would judge others with the same level of intolerance.

It wasn't until my father went on a detour from his perfect behavior, as my mother's husband, that I felt a true liberating feeling. He couldn't demand perfection from me anymore since he was no longer perfect. It made me feel so relieved that I decided to go on a few detours of my own. <wink>

In my own little 19-year-old world I was doing great, I could finally go with the flow, after being such an outlier for most of my life. Perfection wasn't trendy and, in this case, the majority got it right: seeking perfection can damage your health.

We all need time to play, opportunities to make mistakes, to be irresponsible, to not comply with rules imposed by who knows who and to not be so conformist!!

If you've lived under highly demanding standards all your life, when you allow yourself to make mistakes, you feel like a new person. At some point you seek forgiveness, so you learn to forgive.

What kind of mistakes?

"*Yiaya*, what kind of mistakes are you talking about?"

"There's no need to go into the details, Sunday dear. The seriousness of each mistake depends on the code of conduct of each person, which changes with time and geography. I'm referring to mistakes that won't harm your own life or there will be no chance to learn from them. In my case, it was about doing things other kids my age were doing, but my parents wouldn't allow me. Just to give you an example, I wasn't allowed to go to the cinema with my classmates at age 12. My parents considered me to be too young to do so."

"Oh, I see. It's more about having a personal experience you consider forbidden but that it's not considered a bad thing globally."

"Yes, it's like becoming a little bit of a 'bad' person according to a very strict code, so you can tolerate others with a different code from yours. It's the basis for tolerance and compassion. But you have to experience the feeling of helplessness and that need to be forgiven before you can truly forgive others' behaviours that you considered to be wrong. It's all relative."

"It is all relative, *Yiaya*. That is so true!"

Migrant crisis solved

Developing tolerance was imperative in showing compassion towards the many migrants the world had to cope with. There wasn't one single region that didn't get an influx of people coming from a less fortunate place to find some peace and safety.

The members in younger generations were somehow more connected to each other than those in our older generation. They shared entertainment and values at a global scale. Malala Yousafzai had showed the world that there were people who deserved to be helped in countries plagued by extremists.

Focusing on the family was the key to keep terrorism under control. Extremists had mothers, sisters and aunties who wouldn't approve of their intentions of damaging innocent civilians by blowing up themselves in busy areas.

The environment of openness and the welcoming they experienced in countries they considered enemies, were the foundation for love to prevail. In spite of racist comments from government spoke-persons, the citizens came out to welcome tired refugees and offered them shelter and goods. Immigrants were touched by this kindness and some extremists started questioning their views. Eventually they realised their beliefs were the product of growing up immersed in propaganda that twisted the real facts.

Those who had questioned their beliefs started to influence others in their own circles. The snowball of compassion grew. Eventually they all embraced forgiveness and compassion. Only a few were left bitter and resentful but, once they became a minority, they didn't have any power over others to continue with the ball of hatred. Their snowball melted away.

Youngsters raise their voice for causes

Malala Yousafzai was the first of many youngsters who became a symbol for change and hope for a more peaceful and secure world.

After Malala started the education-for-all-girls revolution, there were other teens and young adults who started other revolutions: Cure cancer, be your own spiritual leader, accept sexuality without prejudice and many more. Young voices rose to reach the institutions that had the tools for them to express their ideas, carry out their research or create a group of experts who could best deal with a social prejudice.

Children didn't have to wait to adulthood to fight for their causes. If they published their ideas online they could find sponsors, see their causes taken care of and gain momentum worldwide.

Generational improvements in parenting

I was a more lenient and empathetic parent than my parents were. They had been better parents than their parents and my children were better parents than Alexis and I were. Every new generation, most parents aspire to be the best parents they can be.

Looking back, I can tell you without a doubt that all the mistakes parents make are out of fear. Fear leads to insecurities that could make us too severe on our beloved children. It is hard to let go and to admit that we can only influence them to a point. Their future is in their own hands and we can only hope for the best.

In my case, I believed in prayer because I'd seen my own mother work miracles on us this way. My only fear as a parent was that my children would rather not visit me when they had a choice. I wanted to be a likeable mother to whom her children would want to return to. I understood that I had to serve them with a smile and show how much I loved them so they would want to come back to me in adulthood. I had to be the sweet grandmother I never had.

I purposely focused on the positives of my own parents to find the strength to give more quality time to my children. After all, I had decided to stay home so I could create memories I could remember and, hopefully, the ones they would love reliving too.

We pass on the good, the bad and the ugly

As parents we have to do our best. Every time there is a genetic problem, parents feel guilty. After all, they passed on the genes to their children.

I was astonished when I heard that our children would live less than our parents because of the way we were feeding ourselves. Our children could not build the proteins that fight allergies because we weren't getting the necessary nutrients from our refined foods.

It is now known that children don't only inherit genes from their parents but also the proteins that switch them on. Attention deficits, anxiety, food allergies, it is all controlled by those genes and proteins. We really had to put our patience hats on to help our children overcome their challenges. And when nothing else worked, a prayer would certainly bring peace to all in the family.

I'm sorry to break it to you if you're a young parent: It doesn't matter what you do, your children will all have a different perception of the way you treat them and the things you do for them. Not only that, we all change with time, usually becoming more lenient and tolerant as we become older. This will make your older children complain about how you end up doing things that were not allowed when they were younger.

Sunday poses 2 new questions

"*Yiaya*, I think I understand what you're saying. I find myself questioning my older parents now in my mid 20s in comparison to how they behaved towards me in my teens. How can parents change so much in less than 10 years?"

"Same thing happened to me and my parents after I hadn't seen them for years. I found myself demanding a lot from myself as a young mother, like they had taught me by example, just to find that they themselves were not following what they preached to me. I found them a lot more relaxed, easy going and happy than how I remembered them.

At the beginning, I had a judgemental attitude towards them. I was upset that they had swayed me into acting one way and yet they were doing things differently now. Then one day I realised that, why not? If my parents had changed for the better, I shouldn't be dwelling in the past and following an obsolete code of conduct out of pride.

I remember how they didn't reply to me when I confronted them. I decided to learn from them as a younger adult. It was a luxury they didn't have, since their own parents didn't evolve the same way they had done. It seemed every new generation was learning faster until the current one that seems to have brought all the experiences and wisdom together since birth. I wonder what you will experience in your lifetime, dear Sunday."

"Well, I'll probably be parented by my children, then, ha, ha."

"You're not far from the truth. If I saw that effect between Diego and George, imagine the children that will be born in a few years how advanced they will be. I couldn't see the reason for this difference then, but now I know that George inherited 10 years more of experiences from me and his father than Diego did."

"Cool! You must have felt that kids were born with superpowers as time was passing by."

"Yes, that's exactly how it felt. I had also stopped being a formal 'professional' to become a simple 'housewife' as it was called then. In Greek it sounded worse because, when someone didn't have a formal job, the expression used translates as 'she sits down', 'Κάθεται'. It's not used anymore but it used to."

"No wonder it was so hard to feel good in your own skin being a full time mother and home manager."

"Oh, my darling, that term hadn't made it to the list of acknowledged employments. I hated the words housewife or unemployed which were the categories available when my time to become a home manager came. There was one social platform considered to be the professional one and it gave you ridiculous options if you fell into those categories. There wasn't a system that would consider working in your own home without an income, a legal job. I felt I had no rights to social benefits because I wasn't being officially paid by an employer."

"Wow! Things have really changed, haven't they? Tell me how you managed to upgrade the term to what it is today."

Feel pride on any path you choose

Society as a whole made me feel vulnerable by choosing to stay home and 'being available' to my family. One of my strongest messages as I started The Wave was to make sure that the option to stay home as a parent or just as the available family member would be validated as a job description.

I wasn't happy with the word housewife or stay-at-home mum. I started calling myself a Bio-Statistician in English and a Γεωπόνος in Greek when asked what my profession was. It reflected my academic background. When asked where I was working, I would say, "I work AT home" (as opposed to working FROM home). I didn't want to pretend I was doing something else apart from being full time available to my family.

When asked how I spent my days, I'd describe a bunch of house chores with a proud smile. It took much practice to be able to look at the other person in the eyes and talk about house management tasks in a way that would sound as if I was describing a managerial job position in the corporate world. I had once disregarded conversations about trivial choices made by house managers who were being present in the moment and rather happy, so I was purposely making them sound pompous.

I'd then move on to add that this work option allowed me to save the energy required to deal with the psychology of 2 teenagers and a small child, growing in an era in which people wanted to achieve what, in my humble opinion, was too much. I was from the first parents on this island who had lived through the extra lessons as a child, with music and extra languages added to the school curriculum. I knew that 4 instead of 2 activities weren't going to make a significant difference in our children's lives.

I decided to leave a few free afternoons for my children just to stay home and get bored, if they chose to. It turned out it was a tendency adopted by many parents some 15 years after I did it. They realised that putting their children through all those extra activities was not opening new opportunities for them. It was just creating a bunch of equally qualified and not so creative young adults.

We had to let them fly with freedom and to let them gravitate towards what really attracted them. We learned to look into their abilities and help them decide in the right direction until they were old enough to pursue or quit a certain sport or activity. Overloading them was tiring and stressful, adding to their anxiety rather than contributing in a positive way to their overall development.

We could all feel proud of what we chose to do as the society grew wiser and finally acknowledged the role of a spouse, a parent or a child to someone who needed care, as a valid full time occupation.

Another profession that was vindicated was that of farmers. Their role was put on a pedestal again as they were producing the medicine we were all consuming 3 times a day every single day of our lives. Clean eating was not saving everybody's life but it was healing many and, certainly, increasing quality of life for all.

Other activities were also included in official occupation lists, many of which didn't produce a steady income but would save money to the community. There is no number that can be attached to value certain activities that need to be done on voluntary basis in the community: Helping the elderly to take their medicine, recycling, keeping the public areas clean and so on.

What is important nowadays is that there are valid options for any qualified person to pursue, regardless of whether it is in line with their degree or previous jobs. We can all feel pride on whatever path we choose in life that is of benefit for the community. The value of contribution towards the common good is acknowledged by society at large.

This perfect outcome didn't come without much combined effort from many activists in a time when we could communicate with each other and create a plan. Perseverance and decisiveness played key roles in the accomplishment of our mission, just like with my individual path to happiness.

Hurdles to happiness

In my own love story there were hurdles to overcome. It wasn't all clear and smooth. There were small hurdles that I had to bypass to get to the finish line. They could have persuaded me to go in a different direction but my Alexis was worth the extra effort.

I suppose as with many things in life, the more you work on conquering something, the sweeter the victory. In my case, I just had to overcome my fears and my insecurities. Did I really deserve to be happy? Fate or my God, as I like to call it, had put a book in my hands titled 'You can have what you want'. It sounds obvious yet it is something I needed to read at that particular crossroad in my life.

And so it was. I decided that I would assume all the risks committing to one person entitled. I looked at the challenges in the eye and responded fiercely and decisively. Yes, I wanted to marry this person. Yes, I knew there were hurdles to overcome and risks involved. Time would tell. And it did.

After almost one year of living apart, our love grew bigger and our commitment resulted in me moving to the island with the certainty that it was my ticket to happiness. And it was!

Venezuelans in the Diaspora

I wasn't a Venezuelan living abroad because I fled from a country of horrors. I just happened to meet a wonderful life partner who lived in a land of opportunities at the time and I chose to board the train to happiness with him.

The many Venezuelans-living-abroad phenomenon happened 10-15 years after I had left. Most went to live in Australia, Canada or the United States. Those who were second generation European immigrants could get a passport to their parents' countries and went mainly to Spain, Italy, Portugal and Germany.

My brother Tomas became Irish by his own right after having lived in Ireland since he finished studies in France. He was lucky he left Venezuela in his teens and became truly European in his ways. He was from a selected group of high school leavers who were given scholarships, by the government, to study in any foreign country, for as long as it took, from learning the language and going through the admission process to when they would get their degree.

My brother Luis went to live in Mexico after working opportunities in the oil industry in our oil producing birth country were politicised. He found success there with his family of all Venezuelan girls.

A human phenomenon

The world was full of bilingual or trilingual families due to all the migration waves. The power to be connected to films in all languages helped reinforce the second and third languages in our children.

George, who was the one who lived most of his childhood on the island, could speak Spanish and English fluently besides Greek because he used to watch videos of his favourite animated characters in those languages.

Today, Sunday can connect online and have conversations in Spanish with a Venezuelan accent if she chooses to do so. It's all free and available.

The Bride is ready

"Hi, mum. We're going to Bonaire in 2 weeks. Everything is ready for the Wedding. Diego and Nicole are coming back from London to see you after we leave. Ralph and Sunday will accompany us. George and Susie won't be able to make it. It's the final countdown!"

"I'm so excited for you, Rose. You'll get married in paradise. Who's attending from the Venezuelan family?"

"Tio Luis' daughters are both attending. Tio Tomas' couldn't make it. And also your cousin Laura's daughter, Cristina, will come."

"From the island?"

"We're taking our *koumpari* (Wedding party) and 2 couples from Roy's work."

"Sounds promising. I'm sure you're going to have a lovely day that will be worth remembering forever."

"I truly hope so, mum. I'm so much looking forward to it."

"I'll be enjoying it with you from here. Knowing that you're happy makes me happy. It is your time to shine, take my legacy and enjoy everything life throws at you."

"Thanks, mum. *La bendición.* (Give me your blessing)"

"*Dios te bendiga mi Rosita linda.* (God bless you, my beautiful little Rose)".

Sunday is back from Venezuela

"Hi *Yiaya*. I'm back! I have so much to tell you."

"Hi Sunday dear, it's so good to see you. Your parents have been keeping me company. I managed to stay here until you came back. Tell me all about it. How are Rafael José and Aleena?"

"They're great, *Yiaya*. Guess what? Aleena is pregnant! They're over the moon. The reception at their home went really well. I was introduced as the Greek girl with Venezuelan blood. I must say, I enjoyed the food, the music, dancing. It was all very familiar, as if I'd had been there before. It must have been your genes, *Yiaya*."

"Of course, dear. You felt like home because you *were* home. Yours is the world of your ancestors. Tell me about the Wedding and Bonaire."

"It was spectacular. Once the celebration was over we had time to dive. I saw the most beautiful colours on the reef there. Ralph is a great diver. He also felt at home, *Yiaya*."

"And Yuruani, Angel falls?"

"I didn't want to leave. I fell in love with a toucan, the waterfalls: 'salto la llovizna', 'salto el sapo', one more beautiful than the other. We went up river and arrived at the foot of Angel falls after hiking through the jungle. It was a clear day, so we had a clear view of Auyan Tepui. I've learned all the names, you see?"

"That is fantastic. You're taking me back in time. Yes, Alexi *mou*, we'll be together soon."

"What are you saying? Are you talking to *Pappou* now?"

"I always do, but now that the MRW records everything, you can see it too. I wonder how much I will be able to think after my soul detaches from my body."

"I love you, *Yiaya*. I love you so much."

"Don't cry, dear Sunday. I am done here."

I am done here

I have lived a fortunate life. I was loved and I loved. I could talk about my life and found many sister souls on my path. I am grateful to all my friends and to all of those who cared for what I had to say.

I am sorry for the omissions in my life. I apologise for the times I was judgemental and lacked compassion. I hope you have all forgiven me so that your own path to joy has opened up in front of you.

I am tired of being bed-bound and I must acknowledge I've had the best company from all my children and beloved grandchildren. There isn't anything else you could have done that you didn't do for me. I will always be looking after you, even if you can't read my thoughts anymore.

I want to sleep and dream of Alexis. I miss chatting with my mum. I want to meet my friends who departed before me. There are quite a few that make me want to hurry. I mustn't keep you long and I mustn't keep them waiting.

A letter to Claire

Dear Claire,

You're only a baby today but I already love you so much. There is always a special bond between the grandmother and her granddaughters. You carry some of me in you, even if you won't remember your old *Yiaya* Clara who was bed-bound by the time you were born.

You have your sister Irina and your cousin Sunday who can give you their version of this Venezuelan *abuela* who has contributed to your genome.

As you can see, I'm a Genetics freak. I speak in present tense because who I am and who I was are the same thing. There will never be another one like me, genetically speaking, of course.

You are also unique, my little Claire. And one day you will not be so little anymore but you will be YOU, the same one, the only one. Love yourself and know that you are loved by all your ancestors who feel alive in you.

I would have liked to hold you in my arms and take you to the park but my body is old, only my spirit remains young.

I will hug you from another dimension with my love and I wish you a long and blessed life. One day, in the far future we will be reunited with all the relatives from the island and my birth country.

Take care and listen to your heart.

Love,

Yiaya Clara.

PS: We are '*tocayas*', we have the same name and I hope it brings you much happiness and love like it did to me.

Irina Divina

Darling Irina,

You are the star on stage and *Divina* (Divine) is far from doing you justice. I hope one day you can forgive me for being an absent grandmother.

I do want you to know that I always felt very proud of you, not only for what you have accomplished in your short career as a ballerina, but for who you are.

Who we are is what remains with us forever. If you would allow me to share a small insight from my own experience, I can tell you that even when I've been bed-bound, I've felt much joy by reliving moments of accomplishments in my mind.

Everything you enjoy today and everyday with mindfulness and awareness will remain with you forever.

You are better than all of us, your family on the island and your even more distant relatives from the Venezuelan diaspora. You have a component that we know nothing about.

I am so sorry I didn't devote myself to understanding your mother's life program. I could have been a better mother-in-law while she was married to your father.

I was selfish and I could have certainly done better while they were together. I hope you can forgive my absences and my prejudices.

Now I know better but there is no time. I just wanted you to know how I feel and I trust in your compassion and forgiveness.

Love,

Yiaya Clara.

Last but not least of the girls

Dearest Sunday,

I'm sorry I have to physically go. I want to thank you for having dedicated so much time to our conversations these past months. I enjoyed every single one of them. Your interest kept me going until I felt that I had thought enough.

You are a true star in the space of my life, a very shiny one that I can distinguish from all the others.

I am sure you're going to be a happy and fulfilled woman who will make her own free choices as to what she wants to accomplish in life.

I wish you to find what you long for. If you want a life partner, I wish for you the best.

Children? As many healthy ones as you can handle and enjoy.

Much health and time to look inwards, outwards and all that surrounds you.

I wish much beauty in your life from all the people who approach you, the goods you consume, the music you hear and the colours you see.

Thank you for calling me *Yiaya* Clarita. I loved every one of the times you did.

Goodbye *Kyriaki mou,* (My Sunday)

Dios te bendiga, mi amor. (God bless you, my love).

To the grandsons

Dear Ralph and Anthony,

My dear boys, men are wonderful creatures of few words and your *Yiaya* Clara doesn't have much time.

You came into our lives as bearers of the legacy of your fathers and grandfathers. Your *Pappou* Alexis would be so proud of what you have become. It is my time to join him in another dimension and share what I lived these last 3 years since he departed.

I just want to tell you what I told your uncles and father: let the women in your life guide you when it comes to choosing a woman as a life partner. Your mothers, sisters or cousins can read subtle signs from other women that you can't. Listen to what they have to say but, most importantly, listen to your own intuition and pray. God always knows better.

Now it is my time to go and I wanted to say goodbye. Ralph can tell a few stories to Anthony about me. I will join your *Pappou* in an eternal garden of love and joy. I wish you much happiness in life as we had ourselves.

Farewell, peace, much love,

Yiaya Clara.

Tribute from George

Dear Clara,

You were more than just a mother to me.
You were my friend and my biggest supporter.
I will miss your words, your eyes and your smell.
You will live in my heart forever.
I love you.

I will forever remember when you told me in secret that I was the child you loved the most. It was something I needed to hear and you knew it. Thank you for always making me feel special. You more than made up for those 10 extra years you gave to my eldest brother.

Rest in peace and enjoy dad's company.

Lucky him, who can have the pleasure of your company now.

I hope you'll be looking at us with pride.

Susie, Claire, Anthony, Irina and I will always be indebted to you.

Καλό ταξίδι μαμά! Feliz viaje. Te amamos. (Have a good trip, mum. We love you).

Tribute from Rose

What can I say today that we haven't said before?

You're my inspiration and my sister soul.
You might not be thinking to us anymore but you are embedded in our selves.
Wherever we go, you come with us.
Whatever we do, you do through us.

Clara Diaz, Clara Diaz, we don't need explanations about your name.

You're the best mother, sister, daughter, wife anyone could have asked for.

I'm fortunate to be your daughter.

I love you mummy. Take care and be safe.

Sunday speaks for the grandchildren

I can't believe you won't be thinking to us anymore, *Yiaya* Clara, *Abuelita*.

My heart sinks to the thought of your empty bed. But I know how lonely you must have felt not being able to function properly physically for so long.

We are fortunate you decided to think to us a bit more. I will treasure your words for ever. I will tell my cousins stories about the days when you could move and talk and you played with me. You taught me what it meant to be born in paradise and how we could find paradise everywhere we went.

You will always be my inspiration and my beloved *Yiaya*. I will dream of you and I will hug you at night. Rest in peace and try not to make so much noise in paradise. You'll have the Angels dancing at the rhythm of your music. I will see you in every rainbow I'll come across.

Farewell, *Abuelita*. Love you much.

Bye mum. You will always live in our hearts

I always knew this day would come but I never expected it to be so difficult. It was painful to say goodbye to dad, but we still had you to keep us company.

I enjoyed every day I spent with you. From my early attraction to light and wheels, I never ignored you. I just knew you were there for me.

I hope I didn't disappoint you in being there for you when the circle of life gave me the chance to offer some kind of distraction for your soul.

You invented the colour ceiling device with me. That pretty much summarises what you stood for. You're an innovator and a brave, open minded, compassionate human being who says goodbye to this dimension today.

Bye, mum. Nicole, Sunday and I will keep your memory alive. But please rest in peace, we'll be fine. We will find comfort in knowing that dad and you will be in the same dimension. And I can tell you I enjoy it very much here, but part of me is looking forward to seeing you both again.

Eternal be your memory.

The end

I loved my funeral. Thank you for such a beautiful tribute. I feel so young and strong. There's Alexis with black hair. Hello my love! Bye bye life.

About the author

You can connect with Veronica on Twitter or Instagram at @verowellbeing. She defines herself as an Indie Author who writes to heal and tweets about wellbeing.

Search for Veronica Solorzano Athanasiou on Linkedin or Facebook.

Clara Thinks to Us is now published in Spanish as Los Pensamientos de Clara. You can find it at Amazon.com

Verónica is writing a series in Spanish. It is about letting go of toxic relationships and attitudes to allow for new opportunities in life. The Serie Mejor Sola comprises 5 books. By 2016, 3 books have been published on Amazon, corresponding to the stories of three of four friends who grew up together in an imaginary city that resembles Veronica's birth country, Venezuela.

To the people of Cyprus

I am very grateful for all the years I have lived on this beautiful island. Not being native, I didn't feel worthy of referring to it by its name in this book.

As a sign of respect to all the pain suffered by the refugees who were displaced from their homes in 1974, I refrained from naming a single Cypriot village. I can only imagine how difficult it is to go through such an ordeal.

The Cyprus problem is a very complex one and I didn't want to treat it lightly, so the resemblance in the novel with Clara's island is a way of expressing my true hope that the island will see better days ahead.

Verónica

Acknowledgements

It took a village to write and edit this book. I want to thank my family for their support.

It was a very challenging but fulfilling experience. It is great to be able to write what you feel, think and wish for.

I wish peace and prosperity for both my birth and adoptive lands. I hope all humans can live together in peace and work as one to make our world a better place.

Printed in Great Britain
by Amazon